RENEWING

WORSHIP

SONGBOOK

New Hymns and Songs
for Provisional Use

Evangelical Lutheran Church in America
Published by Augsburg Fortress

RENEWING WORSHIP SONGBOOK

Also available:
New Hymns and Songs: Renewing Worship, vol. 5
(full score companion volume to *Renewing Worship Songbook*)
ISBN 0-8066-7005-3

This resource has been prepared by the Evangelical Lutheran Church in America for provisional use.

The paper used in this publication meets the minimum requirements of American National Standard for Information Sciences—Permanence of Paper for Printed Library Materials, ANSI Z329.48-1984.

Manufactured in the U.S.A.   ISBN 0-8066-7050-9

07   06   05   04   03   1   2   3   4   5

Contents

Preface

In the years since the publication of *Lutheran Book of Worship* in 1978, the pace of change both within the church and beyond has quickened. The past three decades have seen not only a growing ecumenical consensus but also a deepened focus on the church's mission to the world. The church has embraced broadened understandings of culture, increasing musical diversity, changes in the usage of language, a renewed understanding of the central pattern of Christian worship, and an explosion of electronic media and technologies. These shifts have had a profound effect on the weekly assembly gathered around word and sacrament. The present situation calls for a renewal of worship and of common resources for worship, a renewal grounded in the treasures of the church's history while open to the possibilities of the future.

RENEWING WORSHIP

Renewing Worship is a response to these emerging changes in the life of the church and the world. Endorsed by the Church Council of the Evangelical Lutheran Church in America (ELCA) and carried out in partnership by the ELCA Division for Congregational Ministries and the Publishing House of the ELCA (Augsburg Fortress), the Renewing Worship project includes a consultative process intended to develop principles for worship; a series of editorial teams that collect, develop, and revise worship materials for provisional use; and regional conferences for resource introduction and evaluation. The final phase of the process envisions the drafting of a comprehensive proposal for new primary worship resources designed to succeed *Lutheran Book of Worship*.

RENEWING WORSHIP SONGBOOK

This volume is part of the provisional resource phase of Renewing Worship. Collecting congregational song is, of course, only one part of preparing for new primary worship resources. Nevertheless, for many people the hymn section of the worship book is the part that holds the most interest and about which they tend to have the most heartfelt opinions.

It is important to emphasize that this volume is not the complete collection of hymns to be proposed for the worship resources that will replace *Lutheran Book of Worship (LBW)*. This provisional volume is a representative sampling of congregational song offered for testing and evaluation, part of the process of refining the compilation of song to be included in more long-term core resources.

WHAT'S INCLUDED?

A quick look at the contents of this volume reveals that materials from many different time periods are included, even though the majority is from the generation following the publication of *LBW*. The "new hymns and songs" in this collection are defined as materials that are not included in two core Lutheran worship resources, *Lutheran Book of Worship* and *With One Voice (WOV,* 1995).

This provisional volume includes materials commissioned for this collection, materials first published in this collection, materials published in the past twenty-five years since *LBW,* older materials that may be in wide usage but were not in the church's core collections, and, occasionally, materials that appeared in those collections but in a different form.

THE PROCESS OF SELECTION

The New Hymnody editorial team met several times in 2002 to select materials for this provisional collection. The process included identifying current issues related to assembly song, articulating criteria for selection, mining denominationally and independently published collections, issuing a call for submissions of new materials, and selecting a representative sampling for provisional use and wider evaluation.

The initial phase of identifying issues and criteria was greatly aided by the foundations of the Evangelical Lutheran Church in America's 1997 statement on the practice of word and sacrament, *The Use of the Means of Grace,* and, more specifically, the work of the 2001 Renewing Worship consultations as summarized in *Principles for Worship* (Renewing Worship, vol. 2), especially the sections "Language and the Christian Assembly" and "Music and the Christian Assembly."

A few highlights from these guiding principles may be helpful. Some of the issues that singing assemblies face a generation after *LBW* include the continuing decline in musical formation of the young, a growing diversity in the backgrounds and church experiences of those who worship as Lutherans, the proliferation of new hymns and songs in response to new creative impulses and new contexts, the engagement of a wider range of musical genres (including many late 20th century popular styles) than were once common in Lutheran worship, and the sometimes competing values of memory and new theological awareness in the words the church sings.

Among the strategies considered to address these issues, several key principles may be singled out: balance, representation, and commonality. As an example of *balance*, careful selection of texts instead of wholesale revision is a way to balance the desire for language that draws a wider circle of imagery of God with the importance of memory and tradition that connects many generations of God's people. The principle of *representation* recognizes that in a time of the proliferation of assembly song and the desire for more choices, any collection intended for widespread use cannot be comprehensive, but will include significant examples of a broad range of materials. Worshiping communities increasingly use various means to include additional songs in the repertoires that are appropriate to their contexts. The value of *commonality* serves as counterpart to a representative principle: a collection of examples of various strands and styles of congregational song should still be able to be embraced by the breadth of the church and should meet many congregations' basic needs for suitable song across seasons, themes, and the lectionary cycle.

THE SHAPE OF THIS COLLECTION

The editorial team focused primarily on recently written hymns and songs. However, a collection made up only of new and unfamiliar material might be less widely used and therefore less useful as a tool for evaluation. Therefore, this provisional collection includes pieces that will be more immediately accessible to congregations, as well as other generally familiar items that provide a greater breadth and scope to the collection.

As a result, about two-thirds of this collection are songs and hymns selected by the editorial team from over three thousand submissions in addition to hundreds of others examined in published collections. The selection has undergone additional revision and refinement based on the review of the New Hymnody development panel (listed in the acknowledgments section).

The remaining third of the collection are primarily songs and hymns from supplemental worship volumes prepared by the ELCA after *WOV: Libro de Liturgia y Cántico* (1998), a Spanish language worship book; *This Far by Faith* (1999), an African American worship resource; and *Worship & Praise* (1999), a selection of contemporary worship songs. It is hoped that the selections from these resources will bring some of these gifts of song to broader awareness and use. At the same time, many of these materials are already widely known and offer an inviting place of entry for exploring other new hymns and songs.

AN EDITION FOR THE WORSHIPING ASSEMBLY

Renewing Worship Songbook contains songs and hymns in versions appropriate for assembly singing. It is intended to provide a cost-effective way for congregations to participate actively in trying out and evaluating new hymns and songs. Generally, hymns are included with harmony when the music can be sung in harmony. Melody line versions are included for hymns that have accompaniments not designed for singing in harmony. Complete accompaniments for all the hymns and songs, together with study notes and additional indexes, are included in *New Hymns and Songs* (Renewing Worship, vol. 5).

FUTURE DEVELOPMENT OF RESOURCES FOR ASSEMBLY SONG

As the materials in this collection are used and evaluated, the Renewing Worship editorial process continues to work on a proposal for a more comprehensive body of congregational song. The rich treasury of song in *LBW* and *WOV* is being carefully considered, assisted by the responses of a representative sample of over six hundred congregations regarding the hymns in these collections. New materials continue to be submitted and will be considered. Feedback to the strategies and examples included in *Congregational Song: Proposals for Renewal* (Renewing Worship, vol. 1) and the present volume will inform the process. A proposal of hymns and songs to be included in a primary common resource will be prepared in time for the ELCA Churchwide Assembly in August 2005.

EVALUATION

An essential part of Renewing Worship is the evaluation by congregations and their leaders of the proposed strategies and content in these volumes. On the Renewing Worship website (www.renewingworship.org) is an evaluation form that may be used to offer feedback on the individual songs as well as the strategies employed in the collection. Feedback received will help to shape the subsequent stages of the process toward new worship materials.

Come Now, O Prince of Peace

1 Come now, O Prince of peace, make us one bod - y.
2 Come now, O God of love, make us one bod - y.
3 Come now and set us free, O God, our Sav - ior.
4 Come, Hope of u - ni - ty, make us one bod - y.
O - so - sŏ o - so - sŏ, pyong - hwa - ŭi - im - gŭm

Come, O Lord Je - sus, rec - on - cile your peo - ple.
Come, O Lord Je - sus, rec - on - cile your peo - ple.
Come, O Lord Je - sus, rec - on - cile all na - tions.
Come, O Lord Je - sus, rec - on - cile all na - tions.
u - ri - ga han - mom i - ru - ge ha - so - sŏ.

Text: Geonyong Lee, b. 1947; tr. Marion Pope
Music: Ososŏ 6 5 5 6, Geonyong Lee
Text and music © Geonyong Lee

R 102

Keep Your Lamps Trimmed and Burning

1 Keep your lamps trimmed and burn - ing, keep your
2 Dark - er mid - night lies be - fore us, dark - er
3 Lo, the morn - ing soon is break - ing, lo, the
4 Keep your lamps trimmed and burn - ing, keep your

lamps trimmed and burn - ing, keep your
mid - night lies be - fore us, dark - er
morn - ing soon is break - ing, lo, the
lamps trimmed and burn - ing, keep your

lamps trimmed and burn - ing, for this work's al-most done.
mid-night lies be - fore us, for this work's al-most done.
morning soon is break - ing, for this work's al-most done.
lamps trimmed and burn - ing, for this work's al-most done.

Refrain

Chil-dren, don't grow wea - ry, chil - dren, don't grow

wea - ry, chil-dren, don't grow wea - ry, for this work's al-most done.

Text: African American spiritual
Music: KEEP YOUR LAMPS, African American spiritual

Wake, Awake, for Night Is Flying

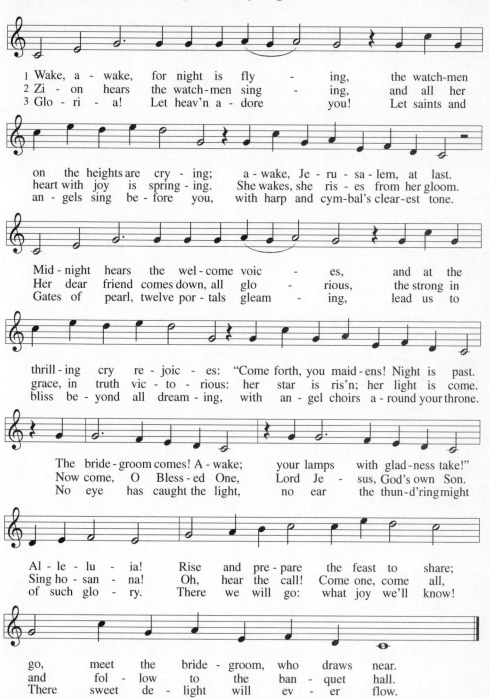

1 Wake, a - wake, for night is fly - ing, the watch-men
2 Zi - on hears the watch-men sing - ing, and all her
3 Glo - ri - a! Let heav'n a - dore you! Let saints and

on the heights are cry - ing; a - wake, Je - ru - sa - lem, at last.
heart with joy is spring - ing. She wakes, she ris - es from her gloom.
an - gels sing be - fore you, with harp and cym - bal's clear-est tone.

Mid - night hears the wel - come voic - es, and at the
Her dear friend comes down, all glo - rious, the strong in
Gates of pearl, twelve por - tals gleam - ing, lead us to

thrill - ing cry re - joic - es: "Come forth, you maid - ens! Night is past.
grace, in truth vic - to - rious: her star is ris'n; her light is come.
bliss be - yond all dream - ing, with an - gel choirs a - round your throne.

The bride - groom comes! A - wake; your lamps with glad-ness take!"
Now come, O Bless - ed One, Lord Je - sus, God's own Son.
No eye has caught the light, no ear the thun - d'ring might

Al - le - lu - ia! Rise and pre - pare the feast to share;
Sing ho - san - na! Oh, hear the call! Come one, come all,
of such glo - ry. There we will go: what joy we'll know!

go, meet the bride - groom, who draws near.
and fol - low to the ban - quet hall.
There sweet de - light will ev - er flow.

Text: Philipp Nicolai, 1556–1608; tr. Catherine Winkworth, 1829–1878, and Martin A. Seltz, b. 1951
Music: WACHET AUF, Philipp Nicolai
Text © 1999 Augsburg Fortress

R 104

Creator of the Stars of Night

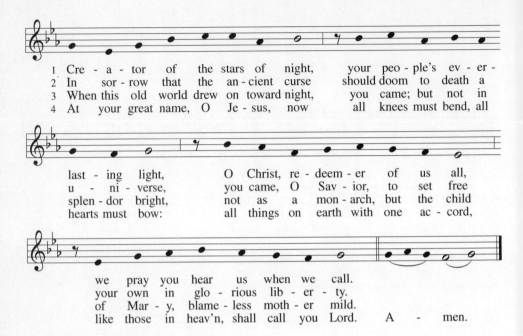

1. Cre - a - tor of the stars of night, your peo - ple's ev - er -
2. In sor - row that the an - cient curse should doom to death a
3. When this old world drew on toward night, you came; but not in
4. At your great name, O Je - sus, now all knees must bend, all

last - ing light, O Christ, re - deem - er of us all,
u - ni - verse, you came, O Sav - ior, to set free
splen - dor bright, not as a mon - arch, but the child
hearts must bow: all things on earth with one ac - cord,

we pray you hear us when we call.
your own in glo - rious lib - er - ty.
of Mar - y, blame - less moth - er mild.
like those in heav'n, shall call you Lord. A - men.

Text: Latin, 9th cent.; vers. *Hymnal 1940*, alt.
Music: CONDITOR ALME SIDERUM   L M, plainsong mode IV
Text © 1940 Church Pension Fund

The King of Glory

Refrain

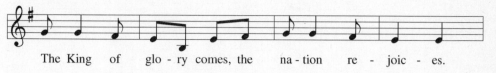

The King of glo - ry comes, the na - tion re - joic - es.

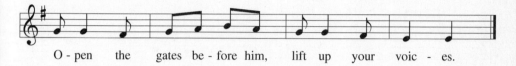

O - pen the gates be - fore him, lift up your voic - es.

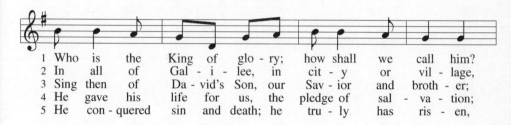

1 Who is the King of glo - ry; how shall we call him?
2 In all of Gal - i - lee, in cit - y or vil - lage,
3 Sing then of Da - vid's Son, our Sav - ior and broth - er;
4 He gave his life for us, the pledge of sal - va - tion;
5 He con - quered sin and death; he tru - ly has ris - en,

Refrain

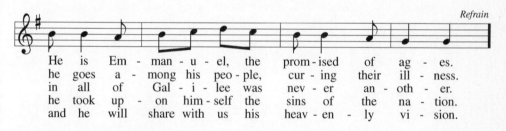

He is Em - man - u - el, the prom - ised of ag - es.
he goes a - mong his peo - ple, cur - ing their ill - ness.
in all of Gal - i - lee was nev - er an - oth - er.
he took up - on him - self the sins of the na - tion.
and he will share with us his heav - en - ly vi - sion.

Text: Willard F. Jabusch, b. 1930

Music: THE KING OF GLORY 12 12 and refrain, Israeli traditional

R 106

There's a Voice in the Wilderness

1 There's a voice in the wil - der - ness cry - ing, a
2 O ... Zi - on, give voice to good tid - ings, as -
3 But your word, O ... God, ... is faith - ful, your

call from the ways un - trod: pre - pare in the des - ert a
cend to the heights and sing! Pro - claim to a des - o - late
arm, O ... Lord, is strong; you stand in the midst of

high - way, a high - way for our God!
peo - ple the com - ing of their king.
na - tions, and you will right the wrong.

The val - leys shall be ex - alt - ed, the
The works of . . . pride all per - ish, like
You will feed your . . . flock like a shep - herd, the

loft - y hills brought low; make straight all the crook - ed
flowers they shall de - cay; the pow'r and . . . pomp of
lambs you'll gent - ly hold; in pas - tures of peace you'll

plac - es where the Lord our God may go!
na - tions shall . . . pass like a dream a - way.
lead them, and . . . bring them to your fold.

Text: James Lewis Milligan, alt., 1876–1961
Music: ASCENSION, Henry Hugh Bancroft, 1904–1988
Music © Estate of Eldred Bancroft

R 107

Magnificat

Text: Luke 1:46, "My soul magnifies the Lord," Taizé Community, 1978
Music: TAIZÉ MAGNIFICAT, Jacques Berthier, 1923–1994
Text and music © 1979 Les Presses de Taizé, GIA Publications, Inc., agent

Pronunciation: mahn-yee-fee-kaht
ah-nee-mah meh-ah doh-mee-noom

Unexpected and Mysterious

R 108

1 Un-ex-pect-ed and mys-te-rious is the gen-tle Word of grace.
2 In a mo-men-ta-ry meet-ing of e-ter-ni-ty and time,
3 We are called to pon-der mys-t'ry and a-wait the com-ing Christ,

Ev-er-lov-ing and sus-tain-ing is the peace of God's em-brace.
Mar-y learned that she would car-ry both the mor-tal and di-vine.
to em-bod-y God's com-pas-sion for each frag-ile hu-man life.

If we fal-ter in our cour-age and we doubt what we have known,
Then she learned of God's com-pas-sion, of E-liz-a-beth's great joy,
God is with us in our long-ing to bring heal-ing to the earth,

God is faith-ful to con-sole us as a moth-er tends her own.
and she ran to greet the wom-an who would rec-og-nize her boy.
while we watch with joy and won-der for the prom-ised Sav-ior's birth.

Text: Jeannette M. Lindholm, b. 1961
Music: JEFFERSON 8 7 8 7 D, W. Walker, *Southern Harmony*, 1835; arr. Donald A. Busarow, b. 1934
Text © 2003 Jeannette M. Lindholm, admin. Augsburg Fortress. Arr. © 1978 *Lutheran Book of Worship*, admin. Augsburg Fortress

R 109

Savior of the Nations, Come

1 Sav - ior of the na - tions, come; vir - gin's son, make
2 Not by hu - man flesh and blood, by the Spir - it
3 Won - drous birth! Oh, won - drous child: might - y cham - pion,

4 From God's heart the Sav - ior speeds, back to God his
5 Now your man - ger's ha - lo bright hal - lows night with
6 Praise we sing to Christ the Lord, vir - gin's son, in -

here your home. Mar - vel now, O heav'n and earth:
of our God was the Word of God made flesh,
in - fant mild, born of Mar - y, God's own Son,

path - way leads, through the gate of death he breaks,
new - born light. Night can - not this light sub - due;
car - nate Word! Praise the Fa - ther and a - dore!

God has cho - sen such a birth.
wom - an's off - spring, pure and fresh.
ea - ger now his race to run!

to God's throne his tri - umph takes.
by your light our faith re - new.
Praise the Spir - it ev - er - more!

Text: Ambrose of Milan, ca. 374; tr. composite
Music: NUN KOMM, DER HEIDEN HEILAND   7 7 7 7, Johann Walter, 1496–1570; arr. Seth Calvisius, 1556–1615
Text © 2003 Augsburg Fortress

Jesus, What a Wonderful Child

Je-sus, Je-sus, Oh, what a won-der-ful child.

Je-sus, Je-sus, so ho-ly, meek, and

mild; new life, new hope the child will bring.

Lis-ten to the an-gels sing: "Glo-ry, glo-ry,

glo - ry," let the heav - ens ring!

Text: African American spiritual
Music: WONDERFUL CHILD, African American spiritual; arr. Jeffrey Radford, 1953–2002
Arr. © 1992 Pilgrim Press, from *The New Century Hymnal*

R 111   Break Forth, O Beauteous Heavenly Light

1 Break forth, O beau - teous heav'n - ly light, and ush - er in the morn - ing;
2 All bless-ing, thanks, and praise to thee, Lord Je - sus Christ, be gi - ven;

ye shep-herds, shrink not with af-fright, but hear the an - gel's warn - ing.
thou hast our broth - er deigned to be, our foes in sun - der riv - en.

This child, now weak in in - fan - cy, our con - fi - dence and joy shall be,
Oh, grant us through our day of grace with con-stant praise to seek thy face;

the pow'r of Sa - tan break - ing, our peace e - ter - nal mak - ing.
grant us ere long in glo - ry with prais - es to a - dore thee.

Text: Johann Rist, 1607–1667; tr. John Troutbeck, 1832–1899, and Arthur T. Russell, 1806–1874
Music: ERMUNTRE DICH 8 7 8 7 8 8 7 7, Johann Schop, 1590–1667; arr. Johann Sebastian Bach, 1685–1750

On Christmas Night

R 112

1 On Christ-mas night all Chris-tians sing to hear the news the
2 Then why should we on earth be sad, since our re-deem-er
3 When sin de-parts be-fore his face, then life and health come
4 All out of dark-ness we have light, which made the an - gels

an - gels bring. On Christ-mas night all Chris-tians sing to
made us glad? Then why should we on earth be sad, since
in its place. When sin de-parts be - fore his face, then
sing this night. All out of dark - ness we have light, which

hear the news the an-gels bring: news of great joy, news of great
our re-deem - er made us glad, when from our sin he set us
life and health come in its place. An - gels re - joice with us and
made the an - gels sing this night: "Glo - ry to God in high-est

mirth, news of our mer - ci - ful king's birth.
free, all for to gain our lib - er - ty?
sing, all for to see the new - born king.
heav'n; peace on earth, and good-will. A - men."

Text: Luke Wadding, d. 1686, alt.
Music: SUSSEX CAROL, English traditional; arr. Ralph Vaughan Williams, 1872–1958

Midnight Stars Make Bright the Sky
Ming-xing can-lan ye wei yang

1 Mid-night stars make bright the skies, Beth-le-hem in slum-ber lies:
2 Mid-night slum-ber lies o'er all, one lone bright lamp lights the stall.

1 Ming-xing can - lan ye wei yang, bo - li - heng cheng zai shui-xiang;
2 Ming-xing can - lan ye wei yang, gu - deng ying - ying zhao ke - chuang;

glis - t'ning heav'n sends forth a great light, shep-herds see a won-drous sight!
Choose old cloth - ing, wrap him warm-ly, man - ger shall his cra-dle be.

ye - wai mu - ren jian yi - xiang, tian-shang jiao-ran fa da-guang;
qu lai jiu - bu zuo qian-pao, ma - cao quan dang yu - er-chuang;

An - gel ranks in cho - rus sing. Silk - en sounds from heav - en ring.
Born to save us from our sin, Word made flesh, our lives to win,

tian - shi lie - dui tong ge - chang, mu - ren jian zhi xian jing - huang;
wei yu jiu - shi zheng xian - ni, dao cheng ren - shen zhen - li zhang;

Fright-ened shep-herds hear them say: Christ is born on earth to - day!
came to earth from heav-en's throne, mor - tals' sin to bear a - lone.

hu - wen lun - yin ban jiu - xiao, xuan - yan Sheng-zi jiang xia-fang:
cai li di - zuo lin xia - jie, ren - shih jian - xin yi bei-chang.

Refrain

Glo - ry be to God on high, blest are all be - neath the sky.
Zhi - gao rong - yao gui Shang-zhu, quan - di ren - min fu wu - jiang.

Text: Jing-qui Yang, 1912–1966; tr. Mildred A. Wiant, b. 1898

Music: HUAN-SHA-XI 7 7 7 7 D and refrain, Qi-fang Liang, b. 1934

Text and music © 1977 The Chinese Christian Literature Council Ltd., Hong Kong

Lo, How a Rose E'er Blooming

1 Lo, how a rose e'er bloom-ing from ten-der stem hath
2 I - sai - ah 'twas fore-told it, the rose I have in
3 This flow'r, whose fra-grance ten - der with sweet-ness fills the
4 O Sav - ior, child of Mar - y, who felt our hu - man

sprung! Of Jes - se's lin - eage com - ing as
mind; with Mar - y we be - hold it, the
air, dis - pels with glo - rious splen - dor the
woe; O Sav - ior, king of glo - ry, who

proph-ets long have sung, it came, a flow'r-et bright, a -
vir - gin moth - er kind. To show God's love a - right, she
dark - ness ev - 'ry - where. True man, yet ver - y God, from
dost our weak - ness know: bring us at length, we pray, to

mid the cold of win - ter, when half-spent was the night.
bore to us a Sav - ior, when half-spent was the night.
sin and death he saves us and light-ens ev - 'ry load.
the bright courts of heav - en, and to the end - less day.

Text: German, 15th cent.; tr. Theodore Baker, 1851–1934, and Harriet R. Krauth, 1845–1925
Music: Es ist ein Ros 7 6 7 6 6 7 6, *Alte Catholische Geistliche Kirchengesäng*, Köln, 1599

Now Let Us Go, O Shepherds
Vamos, pastores, vamos

Refrain / Estribillo

Now let us go, O shep-herds, go to Beth-le-hem.
Va - mos, pas-to - res, va - mos, va - mos a Be - lén

See in the child the glo - ry: E - den a-bloom a - gain.
a ver en e - se ni - ño la glo-ria del E - dén,

See in the child the glo - ry of E - den bloom a - gain.
a ver en e - se ni - ño la glo - ria del E - dén,

See in the child the glo - ry of E - den bloom a - gain, of
a ver en e - se ni - ño la glo-ria del E - dén, la

E - den bloom a - gain, bloom a - gain.
glo - ria del E - dén, del E - dén.

1 Ho - ly and dear-est Je - sus, I give my life to you.
2 Cra-dle with-in a sta - ble, house in an o - pen door,
1 E - se pre-cio - so ni - ño yo me mue - ro por él,
2 Un es - ta-blo es su cu - na, su ca-sa es un por - tal

Hold me with-in your bright eyes, smile here up - on me, too.
straw ver - y rough a pil - low: love came to this, and more.
sus o - ji - tos me en-can - tan, su bo - qui - ta tam-bién.
y so - bre du - ras pa - jas, por nues-tro a-mor es - tá.

Father with soft caresses,
mother with loving care,
lost in a holy wonder,
gaze on you lying there,
gaze on you lying there.

You came a baby, sleeping
next to the ox and mule,
nestled within a blanket,
robe of your royal rule,
robe of your royal rule.

El padre le acaricia,
la madre mira en él:
y los dos extasiados
contemplan aquel ser,
contemplan aquel ser.

Allí duerme el niñito,
cabe un mulo y un buey;
y bien cobijadito,
con un blanco pañal,
con un blanco pañal.

Refrain / Estribillo

3 Wonderful is the Christ child,
lovely beyond compare!
Could any paint or pencil
capture this beauty rare?
For the eternal Father,
infinite pow'r and might,
shares with the Son all glory:
infinite Light from Light,
infinite Light from Light.

3 *Es tan lindo el chiquito
que nunca podrá ser
que su belleza copien
el lápiz ni el pincel.
Pues el eterno Padre
con inmenso poder
hizo que Hijo fuera
inmenso como él,
inmenso como él.*

4 Come to this humble shepherd;
come, Jesus, speak to me,
though I cannot imagine
goodness so kind and free.
Tell me that you forgive me
all, whether great or small;
give me a home eternal
there in your banquet hall,
there in your banquet hall.

4 *Yo pobre pastorcillo
al niño le diré,
no la buena ventura,
eso no puede ser;
le diré me perdone
lo mucho que pequé,
y en la mansión eterna
un ladito me dé,
un ladito me dé.*

Text: E. Ciria, 16th cent.; tr. Martin A. Seltz, b. 1951
Music: VAMOS PASTORES, E. Ciria
Tr. © 2003 Augsburg Fortress

R 116

Love Has Come!

1 Love has come— a light in the dark - ness! Love shines forth in the
2 Love is born! Come, share in the won - der. Love is God now a -
3 Love has come and nev - er will leave us! Love is life ev - er -

Beth - le - hem skies. See, all heav - en has come to pro - claim it;
sleep in the hay. See the glow in the eyes of his moth - er;
last - ing and free. Love is Je - sus with - in and a - mong us.

hear how their song of joy a - ris - es: Love! Love! Born un - to
what is the name her heart is say - ing? Love! Love! Love is the
Love is the peace our hearts are seek - ing. Love! Love! Love is the

you, a Sav - ior! Love! Love! Glo - ry to God on high.
name she whis - pers; Love! Love! Je - sus, Im - man - u - el.
gift of Christ - mas. Love! Love! Praise to you, God on high!

Text: Ken Bible, b. 1950

Music: UN FLAMBEAU 9 9 10 11 9 6, Saboly, 17th cent.; arr. Robert Buckley Farlee, b. 1950

Text © 1996 Integrity's Hosanna! Music/ASCAP

Arr. © 2003 Augsburg Fortress

That Boy-child of Mary

Refrain

That boy-child of Mar - y was born in a sta - ble,
a man-ger his cra - dle in Beth - le - hem.

1 What shall we call him, child of the man - ger?
2 His name is Je - sus, God ev - er with us,
3 How can he save us, how can he help us,
4 Gift of the Fa - ther, to hu - man moth - er,

Refrain

What name is giv - en in Beth - le - hem?
God giv - en for us in Beth - le - hem.
born here a - mong us in Beth - le - hem?
makes him our broth - er in Beth - le - hem.

5 One with the Father,
he is our Savior,
heaven-sent helper
in Bethlehem.

6 Gladly we praise him,
love and adore him,
give ourselves to him,
in Bethlehem.

Text: Tom Colvin, 1925–2000

Music: BLANTYRE 5 5 5 4 and refrain, Malawi traditional; adapt. Tom Colvin

R 118

While Shepherds Watched Their Flocks

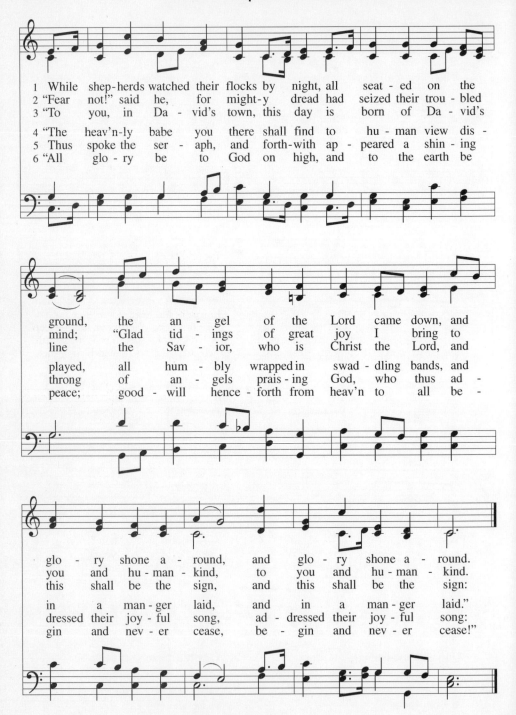

1 While shep-herds watched their flocks by night, all seat - ed on the
2 "Fear not!" said he, for might-y dread had seized their trou - bled
3 "To you, in Da - vid's town, this day is born of Da - vid's
4 "The heav'n-ly babe you there shall find to hu - man view dis -
5 Thus spoke the ser - aph, and forth-with ap - peared a shin - ing
6 "All glo - ry be to God on high, and to the earth be

ground, the an - gel of the Lord came down, and
mind; "Glad tid - ings of great joy I bring to
line the Sav - ior, who is Christ the Lord, and
played, all hum - bly wrapped in swad - dling bands, and
throng of an - gels prais - ing God, who thus ad -
peace; good - will hence - forth from heav'n to all be -

glo - ry shone a - round, and glo - ry shone a - round.
you and hu - man - kind, to you and hu - man - kind.
this shall be the sign, and this shall be the sign:
in a man - ger laid, and in a man - ger laid."
dressed their joy - ful song, ad - dressed their joy - ful song:
gin and nev - er cease, be - gin and nev - er cease!"

Text: Nahum Tate, 1625–1715

Music: CHRISTMAS C M, Weyman's *Melodia Sacra*, 1815; arr. George F. Handel, 1685–1759

See amid the Winter's Snow

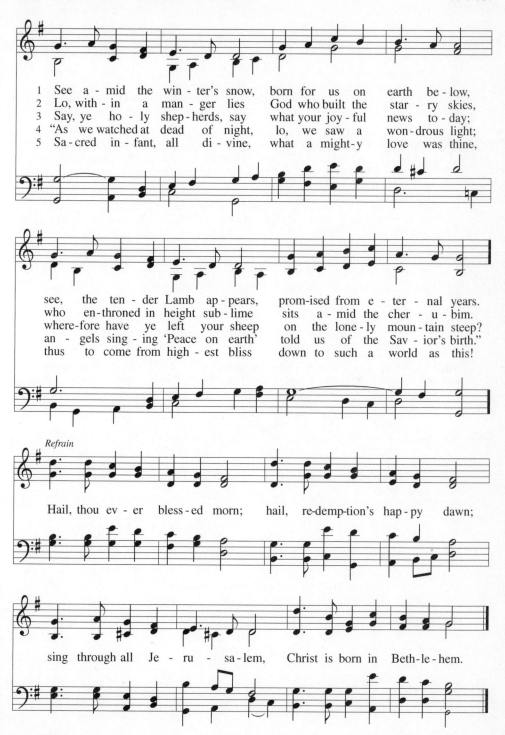

1 See a - mid the win - ter's snow, born for us on earth be - low,
2 Lo, with - in a man - ger lies God who built the star - ry skies,
3 Say, ye ho - ly shep - herds, say what your joy - ful news to - day;
4 "As we watched at dead of night, lo, we saw a won - drous light;
5 Sa - cred in - fant, all di - vine, what a might - y love was thine,

see, the ten - der Lamb ap - pears, prom - ised from e - ter - nal years.
who en - throned in height sub - lime sits a - mid the cher - u - bim.
where-fore have ye left your sheep on the lone - ly moun - tain steep?
an - gels sing - ing 'Peace on earth' told us of the Sav - ior's birth."
thus to come from high - est bliss down to such a world as this!

Refrain

Hail, thou ev - er bless - ed morn; hail, re - demp - tion's hap - py dawn;

sing through all Je - ru - sa - lem, Christ is born in Beth - le - hem.

Text: Edward Caswall, 1814–1878
Music: SEE AMID THE WINTER'S SNOW 7 7 7 7 and refrain, John Goss, 1800–1880

R 120

Where Shepherds Lately Knelt

1 Where shep-herds late-ly knelt and kept the an-gel's word,
2 In that un-like-ly place I find him as they said:
3 How should I not have known I-sa-iah would be there,
4 Can I, will I for-get how love was born, and burned

I come in half-be-lief, a pil-grim strange-ly stirred,
sweet new-born babe, how frail! and in a man-ger bed,
his proph-e-cies ful-filled! With pound-ing heart I stare:
its way in-to my heart un-asked, un-forced, un-earned,

but there is room and wel-come there for me,
a still, small voice to cry one day for me,
a child, a son, the Prince of peace for me,
to die, to live, and not a-lone for me,

but there is room and wel-come there for me.
a still, small voice to cry one day for me.
a child, a son, the Prince of peace for me.
to die, to live, and not a-lone for me?

Text: Jaroslav J. Vajda, b. 1919
Music: MANGER SONG 12 12 10 10, Carl F. Schalk, b. 1929
Text © 1987 Concordia Publishing House
Tune © 1987 Carl F. Schalk

Oh, Sing a Song of Bethlehem

R 121

1 Oh, sing a song of Beth-le-hem, of shep-herds watch-ing there,
2 Oh, sing a song of Naz-a-reth, of days of joy and sun,
3 Oh, sing a song of Gal-i-lee, of lake and woods and hill,
4 Oh, sing a song of Cal-va-ry, its glo-ry and dis-may,

and of the news that came to them from an-gels in the air:
oh, sing of fra-grant flow-ers' breath, and of the Sin-less One:
of one who walked up-on the sea and bade its waves be still:
of one who hung up-on the tree, and took our sins a-way:

the light that shone on Beth-le-hem fills all the world to-day;
for now the flow'rs of Naz-a-reth in ev-'ry heart may grow;
for though, like waves on Gal-i-lee, rough seas of trou-ble roll,
for Christ who died on Cal-va-ry is ris-en from the grave;

of Je-sus' birth and peace on earth the an-gels sing al-way.
now spreads the fame of Je-sus' name on all the winds that blow.
when faith has heard the Sav-ior's word, falls peace up-on the soul.
God's sov-'reign Child, who rec-on-ciled, is might-y now to save.

Text: Louis F. Benson, 1855–1930, alt.
Music: KINGSFOLD C M D, English traditional; arr. Ralph Vaughan Williams, 1872–1958

The Magi Who to Bethlehem Did Go
Los magos que llegaron a Belén

Introduction / Anuncio

The ma - gi who to Beth - le - hem did go were the
Los ma - gos que lle - ga - ron a Be - lén a - nun -

her - alds of the com - ing of Mes - si - ah; and with
cia - ron la lle - ga - da del Me - sí - as, y no -

joy we would al - so has - ten to an - nounce the good news.
so - tros con a - le - grí - a la a - nun - cia - mos hoy tam - bién.

1 From a dis - tant land we come with hum - ble greet - ing,
2 To the new - born child, who has no earth - ly trea - sure,

1 *De tie - rra le - ja - na ve - ni - mos a ver - te,*
2 *Al re - cién na - ci - do que na - ció sin bien - es,*

where the east - ern star our car - a - van is lead - ing.
I have come with gold to bring de - light and plea - sure.

nos sir - ve de guí - a la es - tre - lla de o - rien - te.
o - ro le re - ga - lo pa - ra or - nar sus sien - es.

Refrain / Estribillo

(1–3) Ev - er - shin - ing star, God's bril - liant dawn re -
(4) Glo - ry be to God, who sent the child of

(1–3) *Oh bri - llan - te es - tre - lla que a - nun - cias la au -*
(4) *Glo - ria en las al - tu - ras al Hi - jo de*

veal - ing, ev - er guide our way, God's
hea - ven, glo - ry be to God, and

ro - ra, *no nos fal - te nun - ca*
Dios; *glo - ria en las al - tu - ras*

1–3

pre - sence still as - sur - ing.

tu luz bien - he - cho - ra.

4

peace to all on earth.

y en la tie - rra a - mor.

3 To the child of God
   rich incense I am bringing,
   with aroma sweet
   that heavenward is winging.

4 To the child who came
   to bring us heaven's gladness,
   I have come with myrrh,
   a sign of coming sadness.

3 *Como es Dios el niño*
   le regalo incienso,
   perfume con alas
   que sube hasta el cielo.

4 *Al niño del cielo*
   que bajó a la tierra,
   le regalo mirra
   que inspira tristeza.

Text: Manuel F. Juncos, 1846–1928; tr. Carolyn Jennings, b. 1936
Music: LOS MAGOS 12 12 and refrain, Puerto Rican traditional
Tr. © 1993 Pilgrim Press

R 123   Christ, When for Us You Were Baptized

1 Christ, when for us you were bap - tized, God's Spir - it on you
2 God called you "My be - lov - ed Son"; you are God's ser - vant
3 Straight - way and stead - fast un - til death you then o - beyed the
4 Bap - tize us with your Spir - it, Lord; your cross on us be

came, as peace - ful as a dove, and yet as
true, sent to pro - claim the reign of heav'n, God's
call to serve with free and will - ing heart, to
signed, that like - wise in God's ser - vice we may

ur - gent as a flame, as ur - gent as a flame.
ho - ly will to do, God's ho - ly will to do.
give your life for all, to give your life for all.
per - fect free - dom find, may per - fect free - dom find.

Text: F. Bland Tucker, 1895–1984, alt.
Music: LOBT GOTT, IHR CHRISTEN   8 6 8 6 6, Nikolaus Herman, c. 1480–1561
Text © 1985 The Church Pension Fund

Light Shone in Darkness

R 124

1 Light shone in dark - ness at the world's cre - a - tion,
2 Light shone in dark - ness at the new cre - a - tion;
3 Light shines in dark - ness till the full cre - a - tion;

bath - ing in beau - ty na - ture's rev - e - la - tion. All that has be - ing,
Christ rose in glo - ry, won for us sal - va - tion. Sing, earth and heav - en,
Christ's bo - dy, groan - ing, suf - fers trib - u - la - tion, longs for God's jus - tice,

cry in ad - o - ra - tion, "Praise for the light. A - men!"
hymns of ju - bi - la - tion, praise for the light. A - men!
glob - al trans - for - ma - tion, prays for the light. A - men!

Text: Delores Dufner OSB, b. 1939
Music: LUX IN TENEBRIS 11 11 11 6, Mark Sedio, b. 1954
Text © 2001 Sisters of St. Benedict
Music © 2003 Augsburg Fortress

R 125

The Lord Is My Light

1 The Lord is my light and my sal - va - tion, the
3 Wait on the Lord and be of good cour - age, oh,

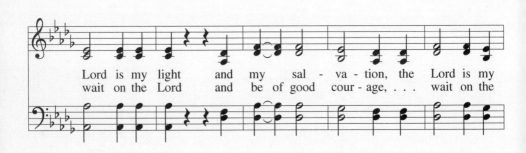

Lord is my light and my sal - va - tion, the Lord is my
wait on the Lord and be of good cour - age, . . . wait on the

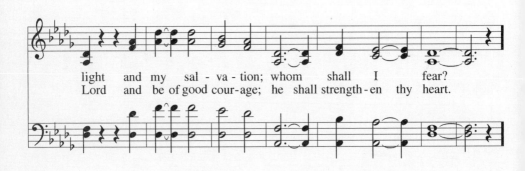

light and my sal - va - tion; whom shall I fear?
Lord and be of good cour-age; he shall strength-en thy heart.

Refrain

Whom shall I fear, whom shall I fear?

The Lord is the strength of my life; whom shall I fear?

2 In the time of trou-ble, he shall hide me; oh, in the time of

trou-ble, he shall hide me; in the time of trou-ble,

D.C. (to stanza 3)

he shall hide me; whom shall I fear?

Text: Lillian Bouknight, based on Psalm 27
Music: THE LORD IS MY LIGHT, Lillian Bouknight; arr. Paul Gainer
Text and music © 1980 Saugos Music, Inc., admin. Malaco Music

R 126

Open the Eyes of My Heart

O-pen the eyes of my heart, Lord. O-pen the eyes of my heart.

I want to see you, I want to see you.

see you. To see you high and lift - ed up,

shin - ing in the light of your glo - ry;

pour out your pow'r and love as we sing "Ho - ly, ho - ly, ho -

ly." - ly."

O-pen the eyes of my heart, Lord. O-pen the eyes of my heart.

I want to see you, I want to see you.

Text and music: Paul Baloche, b. 1962
Text and music © 1997 Integrity's Hosanna! Music/ASCAP

Christ, Be Our Light

1 Long-ing for light, we wait in dark - ness. Long-ing for
2 Long-ing for peace, our world is trou - bled. Long-ing for
3 Long-ing for food, man - y are hun - gry. Long-ing for
4 Long-ing for shel - ter, man - y are home-less. Long-ing for
5 Man - y the gifts, man - y the peo - ple, man - y the

truth, we turn to you. Make us your own,
hope, man - y de - spair. Your word a - lone
wa - ter, man - y still thirst. Make us your bread,
warmth, man - y are cold. Make us your build - ing,
hearts that yearn to be - long. Let us be ser - vants

your ho - ly peo - ple, light for the world to see.
has pow'r to save us. Make us your liv - ing voice.
bro - ken for oth - ers, shared un - til all are fed.
shel - ter - ing oth - ers, walls made of liv - ing stone.
to one an - oth - er, signs of your king - dom come.

Refrain

Christ, be our light! Shine in our hearts. Shine through the

dark - ness. Christ, be our light! Shine in your

church gath - ered to - day.

Text: Bernadette Farrell, b. 1957
Music: CHRIST, BE OUR LIGHT, Bernadette Farrell

R 128

This Little Light of Mine

1 This lit-tle light of mine, I'm goin'-a let it shine;
2 Ev-'ry-where I go, I'm goin'-a let it shine;
3 Je-sus gave it to me, I'm goin'-a let it shine;
oh, oh,

this lit-tle light of mine, I'm goin'-a let it shine;
ev-'ry-where I go, I'm goin'-a let it shine;
Je-sus gave it to me, I'm goin'-a let it shine;
oh,

this lit-tle light of mine, I'm goin'-a let it shine,
ev-'ry-where I go, I'm goin'-a let it shine,
Je-sus gave it to me, I'm goin'-a let it shine,
oh,

let it shine, let it shine, let it shine.
let it shine, let it shine, let it shine.
let it shine, let it shine, let it shine.

Text: African American spiritual
Music: LET IT SHINE, African American spiritual; arr. Horace Clarence Boyer, b. 1935
Arr. © 1992 Horace Clarence Boyer, admin. Augsburg Fortress

Bless Now, O God, the Journey

1 Bless now, O God, the jour - ney that all your peo - ple make,
2 Bless so - journ - ers and pil - grims who share this wind - ing way,
3 Di - vine e - ter - nal lov - er, you meet us on the road.

the path through noise and si - lence, the way of give and take.
whose hope burns through the ter - rors, whose love sus - tains the day.
We wait for lands of prom - ise where milk and hon - ey flow,

The trail is found in des - ert and winds the moun - tain round,
We yearn for ho - ly free - dom while of - ten we are bound;
but wait - ing not for plac - es, you meet us all a - round.

then leads be - side still wa - ters, the road where faith is found.
to - geth - er we are seek - ing the road where faith is found.
Our cov - e - nant is writ - ten on roads, as faith is found.

Text: Sylvia G. Dunstan, 1955–1993
Music: LLANGLOFFAN 7 6 7 6 D, Welsh traditional, Evans' *Hymnau a Thonau*, 1865

R 130

Jesus Is a Rock in a Weary Land

Refrain

Je-sus is a rock in a wea-ry land, a wea-ry land, a wea-ry land; my Je - sus is a rock in a wea-ry land, a shel-ter in the time of storm.

1 No one can do like Je - sus, not a mum-bling word he said; he went walk-ing down to La-z'rus' grave, and he raised him from the dead.

2 When Je - sus was on earth, the flesh was ver - y weak; he gird-ed him-self with a towel and he washed his dis-ci-ples' feet.

3 Yon-der comes my Sav - ior, him whom I love so well; he has the palm of vic-to-ry and the keys of death and hell.

Refrain

Text: African American spiritual
Music: WEARY LAND, African American spiritual

God Will Take Care of You

1 Be not dis - mayed what - e'er be - tide, God will take care of you;
2 Through days of toil when heart doth fail, God will take care of you;
3 All you may need he will pro - vide, God will take care of you;
4 No mat - ter what may be the test, God will take care of you;

be - neath his wings of love a - bide, God will take care of you.
when dan - gers fierce your path as - sail, God will take care of you.
noth - ing you ask will be de - nied, God will take care of you.
lean, wea - ry one, up - on his breast, God will take care of you.

Refrain

God will take care of you, through ev - 'ry day, o'er all the way;

God will take care of you, God will take care of you.
take care of you.

Text: Civilla D. Martin, 1869–1948
Music: MARTIN   C M and refrain, W. Stillman Martin, 1862–1935

R 132   Eternal Lord of Love, Behold Your Church

1 E - ter - nal Lord of love, be - hold your church
2 So dai - ly dy - ing to the way of self,
3 If dead in you, so in you we a - rise,

walk - ing once more the pil - grim way of Lent,
so dai - ly liv - ing to your way of love,
you the first - born of all the faith - ful dead;

led by your cloud by day, by night your fire,
we walk the road, Lord Je - sus, that you trod,
and as through ston - y ground the green shoots break,

moved by your love and toward your pres - ence bent:
know - ing our - selves bap - tized in - to your death:
glo - rious in spring - time dress of leaf and flow'r,

far off yet here— the goal of all de - sire.
so we are dead and live with you in God.
so in - to life and glo - ry shall we wake.

Text: Thomas H. Cain, b. 1931
Music: OLD 124TH   10 10 10 10 10 10, *Trente quatre pseaumes de David*, Geneva, 1551
Text © Thomas H. Cain

Restore in Us, O God

R 133

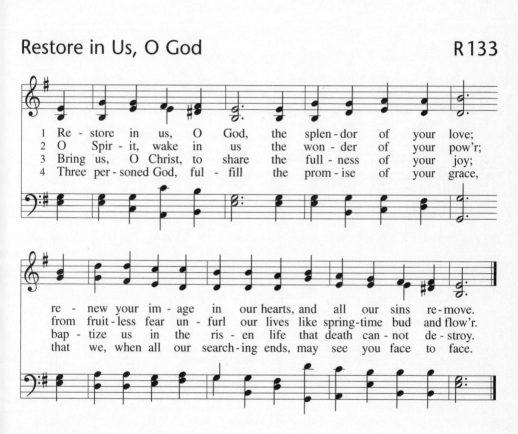

1 Re - store in us, O God, the splen - dor of your love;
2 O Spir - it, wake in us the won - der of your pow'r;
3 Bring us, O Christ, to share the full - ness of your joy;
4 Three per - soned God, ful - fill the prom - ise of your grace,

re - new your im - age in our hearts, and all our sins re - move.
from fruit - less fear un - furl our lives like spring-time bud and flow'r.
bap - tize us in the ris - en life that death can - not de - stroy.
that we, when all our search-ing ends, may see you face to face.

Text: Carl P. Daw Jr., b. 1944
Music: SOUTHWELL   S M, Daman, *Psalmes*, 1579
Text © 1989 Hope Publishing Co. All rights reserved.

R 134

Lamb of God

1 Your on-ly Son, no sin to hide, but you have
2 Your gift of love we cru-ci-fied. We laughed and
3 I was so lost, I should have died, but you have

sent him from your side to walk up-on this guilt-y
scorned him as he died. The hum-ble king we named a
brought me to your side to be led by your staff and

sod and to be-come the Lamb of God.
fraud and sac-ri-ficed the Lamb of God.
rod and to be called a lamb of God.

Refrain

O Lamb of God, sweet Lamb of God, I love the

ho - ly Lamb of God. Oh, wash me in your pre-cious

blood, my Je - sus Christ, the Lamb of God.

Text: Twila Paris, b. 1958

Music: LAMB OF GOD, Twila Paris

R 135

God Loved the World

1 God loved the world so that he gave his on - ly
2 Christ Je - sus is the ground of faith, who was made
3 If you are ill, if death draws near, this truth your
4 Be of good cheer, for God's own Son for - gives all
5 All glo - ry to the Fa - ther, Son, and Ho - ly

Son the lost to save, that all who would in
flesh and suf - fered death; all who con - fide in
trou - bled heart can cheer: Christ Je - sus res - cues
sins that you have done, and jus - ti - fied by
Spir - it, Three in One! To you, O bless - ed

him be - lieve should ev - er - last - ing life re - ceive.
Christ a - lone are built on this chief cor - ner - stone.
us from death; that is the firm - est ground of faith.
Je - sus' blood, your bap - tism grants the high - est good.
Trin - i - ty, be praise now and e - ter - nal - ly!

Text: *Gesangbuch*, Bollhagen, 1791; tr. August Crull, 1846–1923, alt.
Music: ROCKINGHAM OLD L M, adapt. Edward Miller, 1731–1807

As the Deer Runs to the River

1 As the deer runs to the riv - er, parched and
2 When your Is - rael crossed the des - ert where no
3 "Come and drink," I - sa - iah sum - moned, "all who
4 Christ, we come from des - ert plac - es, deep - est

wea - ry from the chase, we have come from hurt and
stream or spring was seen, Mo - ses struck the rock, and
for God's mer - cy plead! God's for - give - ness, like a
thirst un - sat - is - fied. Lead us to the wa - ters

hur - ry, thirst - ing for your heal - ing grace.
wa - ter flowed for them, re - fresh - ing, clean.
foun - tain, flows to sat - is - fy your need."
flow - ing from the cross on which you died.

Je - sus, source of liv - ing wa - ter, may we drink of you and live!

Text: Herman G. Stuempfle Jr., b. 1923
Music: KOMM, O KOMM, DU GEIST DES LEBENS   8 7 8 7 8 7, *Neu-vermehrtes Gesangbuch*, Meiningen, 1693

R 137

Now Behold the Lamb

1 Now be - hold the Lamb, the pre - cious Lamb of God.
2 Ho - ly is the Lamb, the pre - cious Lamb of God.
3 Thank you for the Lamb, the pre - cious Lamb of God.

Bore all my sin, that I may live a - gain: the pre - cious Lamb of God.
Why you love me so, Lord, I shall nev - er know; the pre - cious Lamb of God.
Be - cause of your grace I can fin - ish the race; the pre - cious Lamb of God.

Text: Kirk Franklin, b. 1970
Music: NOW BEHOLD THE LAMB, Kirk Franklin; arr. Keith Hampton

Jesus, Keep Me Near the Cross

R138

1 Je - sus, keep me near the cross, there's a pre - cious foun - tain;
2 Near the cross, a trem - bling soul, love and mer - cy found me;
3 Near the cross! O Lamb of God, bring its scenes be - fore me;
4 Near the cross I'll watch and wait, hop - ing, trust - ing ev - er,

free to all, a heal - ing stream flows from Cal - v'ry's moun - tain.
there the bright and Morn - ing Star sheds its beams a - round me.
help me walk from day to day with its shad - ows o'er me.
till I reach the gold - en strand just be - yond the riv - er.

Refrain

In the cross, in the cross be my glo - ry ev - er;

till my ran - somed soul shall find rest be - yond the riv - er.

Text: Fanny J. Crosby, 1820–1915
Music: NEAR THE CROSS 7 6 7 6 and refrain, William H. Doane, 1832–1915

R 139

Tree of Life and Awesome Mystery

1 Tree of Life and awe - some mys - t'ry, in your
2 We re - mem - ber truth once spo - ken, love passed
3 Christ, you lead and we shall fol - low, stum - bling

death we are re - born; though you die in all of
on through act and word; ev - 'ry per - son lost and
though our steps may be; one with you in joy and

his - t'ry, still you rise with ev - 'ry morn, still you
bro - ken wears the bod - y of our Lord, still you
sor - row, we the riv - er, you the sea, we the

rise with ev - 'ry morn.
bod - y of our Lord.
riv - er, you the sea.

One of the following may be sung as a final stanza at the appropriate time:

General
Light of life beyond conceiving,
mighty Spirit of our Lord;
give new strength to our believing,
give us faith to live your word,
give us faith to live your word.

Lent 1
From the dawning of creation
you have loved us as your own;
stay with us through all temptation,
make us turn to you alone,
make us turn to you alone.

Lent 2
In our call to be a blessing,
may we be a blessing true;
may we live and die confessing
Christ as Lord of all we do,
Christ as Lord of all we do.

Lent 3
Living Water of salvation,
be the fountain of each soul;
springing up in new creation,
flow in us and make us whole,
flow in us and make us whole.

Lent 4
Give us eyes to see you clearly;
make us children of your light.
Give us hearts to live more nearly
as your gospel shining bright,
as your gospel shining bright.

Lent 5
God of all our fear and sorrow,
God who lives beyond our death,
hold us close through each tomorrow,
love as near as every breath,
love as near as every breath.

Text: Marty Haugen, b. 1950
Music: THOMAS   8 7 8 7 7, Marty Haugen

Filled with Excitement

Mantos y palmas

1 Filled with ex - cite - ment, all the hap - py throng
2 As in that en - trance to Je - ru - sa - lem,
1 *Man - tos y pal - mas es - par - cien - do va*
2 *Co - mo_en la_en - tra - da de Je - ru - sa - lén,*

spread cloaks and branch - es on the cit - y streets.
ho - san - nas we will sing to Je - sus Christ,
el pue - blo_a - le - gre de Je - ru - sa - lén,
to - dos can - ta - mos a Je - sús, el rey,

There in the dis - tance they be - gin to see,
to our re - deem - er who still calls to - day,
a - llá_a lo le - jos se_em - pie - za_a mi - rar
al Cris - to vi - vo que nos lla - ma hoy

there on a don - key comes the Son of God.
asks us to fol - low with our love and faith.
en un po - lli - no al Hi - jo de Dios.
pa - ra se - guir - le con a - mor y fe.

Refrain

From ev - 'ry cor - ner a thou-sand voic - es sing
Mien - tras, mil vo - ces re - sue - nan por do-quier: Ho -

praise to the one who comes in the name of God.
san - na_al que vie - ne_en el nom - bre del Se - ñor.

With one great shout of ac - cla-ma-tion loud, tri - um - phant song breaks
Con un a - lien - to de gran ex - cla-ma - ción pro - rrum-pen con voz triun -

forth: Ho - san - na! Ho - san-na to the king!
fal: ¡Ho - san - na! ¡Ho - san - na_al rey!

Ho - san - na! Ho - san - na to the king!
¡Ho - san - na! ¡Ho - san - na_al rey!

Text: Rubén Ruiz Avila, b. 1945; tr. Gertrude C. Suppe, b. 1911

Music: HOSANNA 10 10 10 10, Rubén Ruiz Avila

R141
O Dearest Lord, Your Sacred Head

1 O dear-est Lord, your sa - cred head with thorns was pierced for me:
2 O dear-est Lord, your sa - cred hands with nails were pierced for me:
3 O dear-est Lord, your sa - cred feet with nails were pierced for me:
4 O dear-est Lord, your sa - cred heart with spear was pierced for me:

pour out your bless-ing on my head, that yours my thoughts may be.
pour out your bless-ing on my hands, that yours my work may be.
pour out your bless-ing on my feet, that yours my path may be.
pour out your Spir - it in my heart, that yours my life may be.

Text: Henry Hardy, 1869–1946; rev. Jubilate Hymns Group
Music: DETROIT   C M, *The Sacred Harp*, Philadelphia, 1844; arr. Charles R. Anders, b. 1929
Text © 1982 Jubilate Hymns, admin. Hope Publishing Co. All rights reserved.
Arr. © 1978 *Lutheran Book of Worship*, admin. Augsburg Fortress

When I Survey the Wondrous Cross

R 142

1. When I sur - vey the won - drous cross on which the prince of glo - ry died, my rich-est gain I count but loss and pour con - tempt on all my pride.

2. For - bid it, Lord, that I should boast save in the death of Christ, my God; all the vain things that charm me most, I sac - ri - fice them to his blood.

3. See, from his head, his hands, his feet, sor - row and love flow min - gled down. Did e'er such love and sor - row meet, or thorns com - pose so rich a crown?

4. Were the whole realm of na - ture mine, that were a trib - ute far too small; love so a - maz - ing, so di - vine, de - mands my soul, my life, my all.

Text: Isaac Watts, 1674–1748
Music: HAMBURG   L M, Lowell Mason, 1792–1872

R 143

Calvary

Cal - va - ry, Cal - va - ry, Cal - va - ry,

Cal - va - ry, Cal - va - ry, Cal - va -

ry, sure - ly he died on Cal - va - ry.

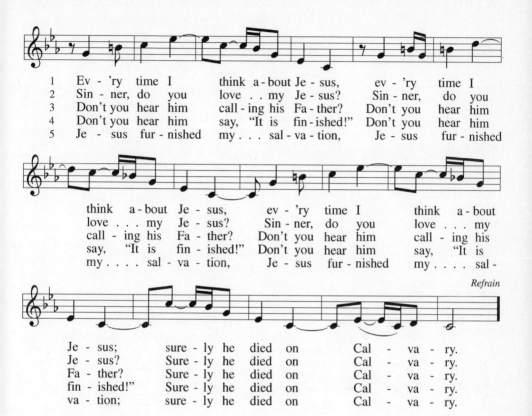

1 Ev - 'ry time I think a - bout Je - sus, ev - 'ry time I
2 Sin - ner, do you love . . my Je - sus? Sin - ner, do you
3 Don't you hear him call - ing his Fa - ther? Don't you hear him
4 Don't you hear him say, "It is fin - ished!" Don't you hear him
5 Je - sus fur - nished my . . . sal - va - tion, Je - sus fur - nished

think a - bout Je - sus, ev - 'ry time I think a - bout
love . . . my Je - sus? Sin - ner, do you love . . . my
call - ing his Fa - ther? Don't you hear him call - ing his
say, "It is fin - ished!" Don't you hear him say, "It is
my . . . . sal - va - tion, Je - sus fur - nished my . . . . sal -

Refrain

Je - sus; sure - ly he died on Cal - va - ry.
Je - sus? Sure - ly he died on Cal - va - ry.
Fa - ther? Sure - ly he died on Cal - va - ry.
fin - ished!" Sure - ly he died on Cal - va - ry.
va - tion; sure - ly he died on Cal - va - ry.

Text: African American spiritual
Music: CALVARY, African American spiritual

R 144

They Crucified My Lord

1 They cru - ci - fied my Lord, and he nev - er said a mum-ba-lin' word;
2 They nailed him to a tree, and he nev - er said a mum-ba-lin' word;
3 They pierced him in the side, and he nev - er said a mum-ba-lin' word;
4 The blood came stream-in' down, and he nev - er said a mum-ba-lin' word;
5 He hung his head and died, and he nev - er said a mum-ba-lin' word;

they cru - ci - fied my Lord, and he nev - er said a mum-ba-lin' word;
they nailed him to a tree, and he nev - er said a mum-ba-lin' word;
they pierced him in the side, and he nev - er said a mum-ba-lin' word;
the blood came stream-in' down, and he nev - er said a mum-ba-lin' word;
he hung his head and died, and he nev - er said a mum-ba-lin' word;

not a word, not a word, not a word.

Text: African American spiritual
Music: SUFFERER   6 10 6 10 9, African American spiritual

The Risen Christ

1 The ris-en Christ, who walks on wound-ed feet
2 The ris-en Christ, who stands with wound-ed side,
3 The ris-en Christ, who breaks with wound-ed hand
4 May we, Christ's bod - y, walk and serve and stand

from gar - den tomb through dark-ened cit - y street,
breathes out his Spir - it on them to a - bide,
the bread for those who fail to un - der - stand,
with the op - pressed in this and ev - 'ry land,

un - locks the door of grief, de - spair, and fear,
whose faith still wa - vers, who dare not be - lieve,
re - veals him - self, de - spite their lin - g'ring tears,
till all are blessed and can a bless - ing be,

and speaks a word of peace to all who hear.
new grace, new strength, new pur - pose they re - ceive.
en - flames their hearts, then quick - ly dis - ap - pears.
re - stored in Christ to true hu - man - i - ty.

Text: Nigel Weaver, b. 1952

Music: WOODLANDS 10 10 10 10, Walter Greatorex, 1877–1949

Text © 1993 Nigel Weaver

Music © Oxford University Press

Alleluia! Christ Is Arisen
¡Aleluya! Cristo resucitó

Refrain / Estribillo

Al - le - lu - ia! Christ is a - ris - en.
¡A - le - lu - ya! Cris - to re - su - ci - tó

Bright is the dawn-ing of the Lord's day.
de ma - dru - ga - da el do - min - go.

1 Run, faith - ful wom-en, to the grave-side.   Mar - vel, the
2 Rise, Mag - da - len - a, from your weep-ing;   Christ stands be -

1 Fue - ron mu - jer-es al se - pul - cro.   Le pie - dra un
2 La Mag - da - le - na fue a llo - rar - lo   y Cris - to

stone is rolled a - way!   Hear from the an - gel, "He is
fore your ver - y eyes.   Quick - ly re - turn to the dis -

án - gel re - mo - vió;   les di - jo: "Ha re - su - ci -
se le a - pa - re - ció;   le pi - dió ir a sus her -

Refrain / Estribillo

ris - en."   Christ goes be - fore you all the way.
ci - ples;   bear the good news: "He is a - live."

ta - do."   Y al ir - se, les sa - lió el Se - ñor.
ma - nos   con un en - car - go que le dio.

3 Gather, disciples, in the evening:
   suddenly Christ your Lord appears.
   "Look, it is I, your wounded Savior.
   Peace be with you, and do not fear."

3 A los discípulos, de tarde,
   Cristo también se presentó.
   Les enseño las cinco heridas;
   dando la paz los saludó.

4 Thomas, where were you on that evening?
   "I'll not believe unless I see."
   Christ comes again, and ev'ry Lord's day:
   "Touch me and see; have faith in me."

4 Tomás no estaba en ese encuentro;
   y ver, pidió, para creer.
   Cristo volvió, le dijo: "Mira,
   palpa mi herida y ten fe."

Text: Luis Bojos; tr. Martin A. Seltz, b. 1951
Music: SANTO DOMINGO 9 8 9 8 and refrain, Luis Bojos
Spanish text and tune © Luis Bojos
English text © 2003 Augsburg Fortress

That Easter Day with Joy Was Bright

1 That Eas - ter day with joy was bright; the
2 O Je - sus, king of gen - tle - ness, with
3 O Christ, you are the Lord of all in
4 All praise, O ris - en Lord, we give to

sun shone out with fair - er light, Al - le -
con - stant love our hearts pos - sess. Al - le -
this our Eas - ter fes - ti - val, Al - le -
you, once dead, but now a - live! Al - le -

lu - ia! Al - le - lu - ia! when, to their long - ing eyes re -
lu - ia! Al - le - lu - ia! To you our lips will ev - er
lu - ia! Al - le - lu - ia! for you will be our strength and
lu - ia! Al - le - lu - ia! To God the Fa - ther e - qual

stored, the a - pos - tles saw their ris - en
raise the trib - ute of our grate - ful
shield from ev - 'ry weap - on death can
praise, and God the Ho - ly Ghost, we

Lord! Al - le - lu - ia! Al - le - lu - ia! Al - le -
praise. Al - le - lu - ia! Al - le - lu - ia! Al - le -
wield. Al - le - lu - ia! Al - le - lu - ia! Al - le -
raise! Al - le - lu - ia! Al - le - lu - ia! Al - le -

lu - ia, al - le - lu - ia, al - le - lu - ia!
lu - ia, al - le - lu - ia, al - le - lu - ia!
lu - ia, al - le - lu - ia, al - le - lu - ia!
lu - ia, al - le - lu - ia, al - le - lu - ia!

Text: Latin, 4th or 5th cent.; tr. John M. Neale, 1818–1866
Music: LASST UNS ERFREUEN 8 8 8 8 8 8 and alleluias, *Geistliche Kirchengesänge*, Köln, 1623

R 148

Christ Is Risen! Shout Hosanna

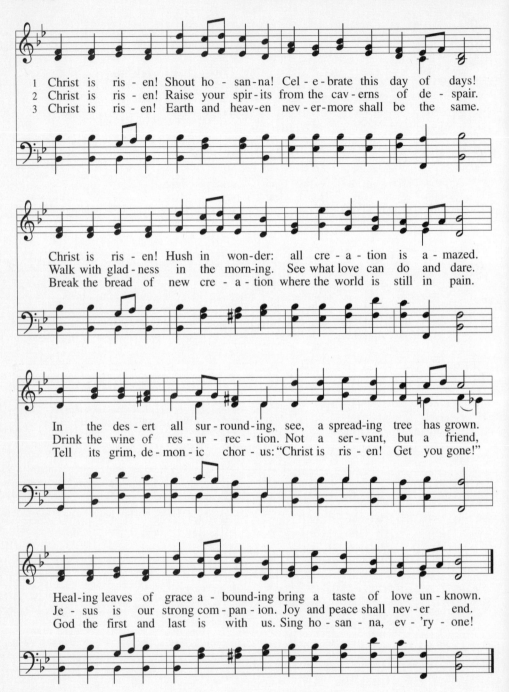

1 Christ is ris - en! Shout ho - san - na! Cel - e - brate this day of days!
2 Christ is ris - en! Raise your spir - its from the cav - erns of de - spair.
3 Christ is ris - en! Earth and heav - en nev - er - more shall be the same.

Christ is ris - en! Hush in won - der: all cre - a - tion is a - mazed.
Walk with glad - ness in the morn - ing. See what love can do and dare.
Break the bread of new cre - a - tion where the world is still in pain.

In the des - ert all sur - round - ing, see, a spread - ing tree has grown.
Drink the wine of res - ur - rec - tion. Not a ser - vant, but a friend,
Tell its grim, de - mon - ic chor - us: "Christ is ris - en! Get you gone!"

Heal - ing leaves of grace a - bound - ing bring a taste of love un - known.
Je - sus is our strong com - pan - ion. Joy and peace shall nev - er end.
God the first and last is with us. Sing ho - san - na, ev - 'ry - one!

Text: Brian A. Wren, b. 1936
Music: BEECHER 8 7 8 7 D, John Zundel, 1815–1882

Day of Arising

1 Day of a - ris - ing, Christ on the road - way,
2 When we are walk - ing, doubt - ful and dread - ing,
3 Lo, I am with you, Je - sus has spo - ken,
4 Christ, our com - pan - ion, hope for the jour - ney,

un - known com - pan - ion walks with his own.
blind - ed by sad - ness, slow - ness of heart,
this is Christ's prom - ise, this is Christ's sign:
bread of com - pas - sion, o - pen our eyes.

When they in - vite him, as fades the first day,
yet Christ walks with us, ev - er a - wait - ing
when the church gath - ers, when bread is bro - ken,
Grant us your vi - sion, set all hearts burn - ing

and bread is bro - ken, Christ is made known.
our in - vi - ta - tion: Stay, do not part.
there Christ is with us in bread and wine.
that all cre - a - tion with you may rise.

Text: Susan Palo Cherwien, b. 1953

Music: Raabe   5 5 5 4 D, Carl F. Schalk, b. 1929

Text © 1996 Susan Palo Cherwien, admin. Augsburg Fortress

Music © 1999 Augsburg Fortress

Up from the Grave He Arose

1 Low in the grave he lay, Je - sus my Sav - ior,
2 Vain - ly they watch his bed, Je - sus my Sav - ior;
3 Death can - not keep its prey, Je - sus my Sav - ior;

wait - ing the com - ing day, Je - sus my Lord.
vain - ly they seal the dead, Je - sus my Lord.
he tore the bars a - way, Je - sus my Lord.

Refrain

Up from the grave he a - rose, with a
he a - rose,

might - y tri - umph o'er his foes; he a -
o'er his foes,

rose a vic - tor o - ver death's do - main, and he

lives for - ev - er, with his saints to reign. He a -

rose! He a - rose! Hal - le - lu - jah! Christ a - rose!

He a - rose! He a - rose!

Text: Robert Lowry, 1826–1899
Music: CHRIST AROSE   6 5 6 4 and refrain, Robert Lowry

R 151

Blessing, Honor, and Glory

Bless - ing, hon - or, glo - ry to the Lamb.

Ho - ly, righ - teous, wor - thy is the Lamb.

Death could not hold him down, for he is ris - en!

Seat - ed up - on the throne, he is the Lamb of God!

God! Bless - ing, hon - or, glo - ry to the Lamb.

Ho - ly, righ - teous, wor - thy is the Lamb of God.

Text: Geoff Bullock and David Reidy

Music: BLESSING, HONOR, AND GLORY, Geoff Bullock and David Reidy

Holy Spirit, Rain Down

R 152

Text: Russell Fragar

Music: Rain Down, Russell Fragar

Text and music © 1997 Russell Fragar/Hillsong Publishing, admin. in the U.S. & Canada by Integrity's Hosanna! Music

R 153

Send Down the Fire

Refrain

Send down the fire of your jus-tice, send down the rains of your love; come, send down the Spir-it, breathe life in your peo-ple, and we shall be peo-ple of God.

1 Call us to be your com - pas - sion,
2 Call us to learn of your mer - cy,
3 Call us to an - swer op - pres - sion,
4 Call us to wit - ness your king - dom,

teach us the song of your love; give us hearts that
teach us the way of your peace; give us hearts that
teach us the fire of your truth; give us righ - teous
give us the pres - ence of Christ; may your ho - ly

sing, give us deeds that ring, make us
feel, give us hands that heal, make us
souls, till your jus - tice rolls, make us
light keep us shin - ing bright, ev - er

To refrain

ring with the song of your love.
walk in the way of your peace.
burn with the fire of your truth.
shine with the pres - ence of Christ.

Text: Marty Haugen, b. 1950

Music: SEND DOWN THE FIRE, Marty Haugen

Fire of God, Undying Flame

R154

1 Fire of God, un-dy-ing flame, Spir-it who in splen-dor came,
2 Strength of God, your might with-in con-quers sor-row, pain, and sin.

let your heat my soul re-fine till it glows with love di-vine.
For-ti-fy from e-vil's art all the gate-ways of my heart.

Breath of God, that swept in pow'r in the pen-te-cos-tal hour,
Love of God, your grace pro-found knows not ei-ther age or bound.

ho-ly breath, be now in me source of vi-tal en-er-gy.
Come, my heart's own guest to be; dwell for-ev-er-more in me.

Text: Albert F. Bayly, 1901–1984
Music: ABERYSTWYTH 7 7 7 7 D, Joseph Parry, 1841–1903

R 155

Give Thanks for Saints

1 Give thanks for those whose faith is firm when all a-round seems
2 Give thanks for those whose hope is clear, be-yond mere mor-tal
3 Give thanks for those whose love is pure, a spar-kling pre-cious
4 Give thanks for saints of a-ges past and saints a-live to-

bleak: on God's good prom-ise they re-ly, so
sight: who seek the cit-y God has planned, the
stone: they show by what they say and do an
day: though of-ten by this world de-spised, their

while they live and when they die how force-ful-ly they
true, e-ter-nal prom-ised land, and steer to-ward that
in-ward beau-ty, warm and true, for God's con-cerns they
hearts by God are rich-ly prized. Give thanks that we may

speak— the strong, who once were weak!
light, a bea-con ev-er bright.
own— God's love through them is known.
say we share their pil-grim way.

Text: Martin E. Leckebusch, b. 1962
Music: REPTON 8 6 8 8 6 6, C. Hubert H. Parry, 1848–1918
Text © 2003 Kevin Mayhew Ltd.

Christ Is the King!

1 Christ is the king! O friends, re - joice;
2 Oh, mag - ni - fy the Lord, and raise
3 O Chris - tian wom - en, Chris - tian men,
4 Let love's all - rec - on - cil - ing might
5 So shall the church at last be one;

broth - ers and sis - ters, with one voice
an - thems of joy and ho - ly praise
all the world o - ver, seek a - gain
your scat - tered com - pa - nies u - nite
so shall God's will on earth be done,

let the world know he is your choice.
for all his saints of an - cient days.
the way his faith - ful fol - lowed then.
in ser - vice to the Lord of light.
new lamps be lit, new tasks be - gun.

Al - le - lu - ia, al - le - lu - ia, al - le - lu - ia!

Text: George K. A. Bell, alt., 1883–1958
Music: GELOBT SEI GOTT   8 8 8 and alleluias, Melchior Vulpius, c. 1570–1615

R 157

O Christ, What Can It Mean for Us

1 O Christ, what can it mean for us to claim you as our king? What roy - al face have you re - vealed whose praise the church would sing? As - pir - ing not to glo - ry's height, to pow - er, wealth and fame, you

2 You came, the im - age of our God, to heal and to for - give, to shed your blood for sin - ners' sake that we might rise and live. To break the law of death you came, the law of love to bring: a

3 Though some would make their great - ness felt and lord it o - ver all, you said the first must be the last and ser - vice be our call. O Christ, in work - place, church, and home, let none to pow - er cling; for

4 You chose a hum - ble hu - man form and shunned the world's re - nown; you died for us up - on a cross with thorns your on - ly crown. But still, be - yond the span of years, our glad ho - san - nas ring, for

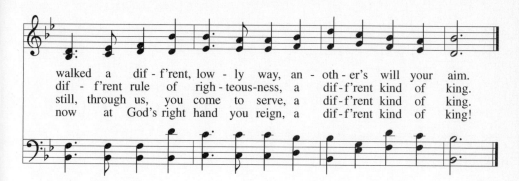

walked a dif-f'rent, low-ly way, an-oth-er's will your aim.
dif-f'rent rule of righ-teous-ness, a dif-f'rent kind of king.
still, through us, you come to serve, a dif-f'rent kind of king.
now at God's right hand you reign, a dif-f'rent kind of king!

Text: Delores Dufner OSB, b. 1939
Music: ALL SAINTS NEW   C M D, Henry S. Cutler, 1824–1902
Text © 2001 Sisters of St. Benedict

Crashing Waters at Creation   R 158

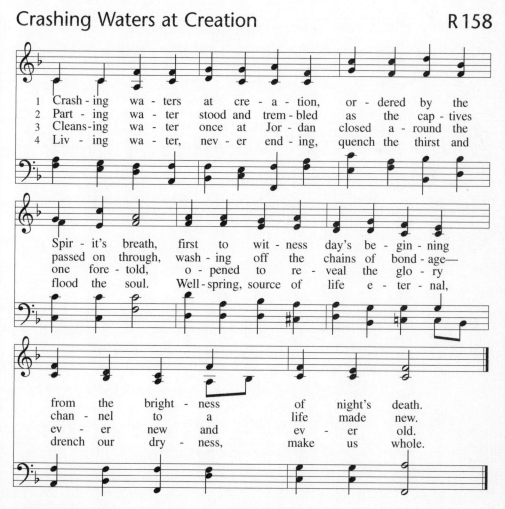

1 Crash-ing wa-ters at cre-a-tion, or-dered by the
2 Part-ing wa-ter stood and trem-bled as the cap-tives
3 Cleans-ing wa-ter once at Jor-dan closed a-round the
4 Liv-ing wa-ter, nev-er end-ing, quench the thirst and

Spir-it's breath, first to wit-ness day's be-gin-ning
passed on through, wash-ing off the chains of bond-age—
one fore-told, o-pened to re-veal the glo-ry
flood the soul. Well-spring, source of life e-ter-nal,

from the bright-ness of night's death.
chan-nel to a life made new.
ev-er new and ev-er old.
drench our dry-ness, make us whole.

Text: Sylvia G. Dunstan, 1955–1993
Music: STUTTGART   8 7 8 7, attr. Christian F. Witt, 1660–1716; adapt. Henry J. Gauntlett, 1805–1876
Text © 1994 GIA Publications, Inc. All rights reserved.

R 159

Wade in the Water

Text: African American spiritual
Music: WADE IN THE WATER, African American spiritual; arr. Carl Haywood, b. 1949
Arr. from *The Haywood Collection of Negro Spirituals* © 1992 Carl Haywood

Song over the Waters

R 160

Refrain

God, you have moved up - on the wa - ters, you have sung in the
rush of wind and flame; and in your love you have called us sons and
daugh-ters, make us peo - ple of the wa - ter and your name.

A

1 Come fill our wait-ing hearts with the spir - it of
2 Give us a thirst for love, give us a hun - ger for
3 You are the breath of life, you are the hope of the
4 Come, o - pen ev - 'ry heart, come now and wake us to

Refrain

Je - sus, let us shine with your light and peace.
jus - tice, make us one with the mind of Christ.
hope - less, come and fill us with light and peace.
won - der, make us ves - sels of light and peace.

B Leader · All

Wa - ters of the sea, wa - ters of the earth: Re - new us!
Riv - ers of the earth, gen - tle flow-ing streams: Re - new us!
Wa - ters of the clouds, wa - ters of the wind: Re - new us!
Might-y blow-ing storms, gen - tle fall - ing rains: Re - new us!

Leader · All

*repeat as needed,
then to refrain*

Wa - ters of the skies, wa - ters of our birth: Re - new us!
Spir - it of our hopes, spir - it of our dreams: Re - new us!
Wa - ters that will be, wa - ters that have been: Re - new us!
Wa - ter for the vine, wa - ter for the grain: Re - new us!

Text: Marty Haugen, b. 1950
Music: SONG OVER THE WATERS, Marty Haugen

R 161

Waterlife

1 Be - fore I can re-mem-ber the cov - e - nant was sealed
2 A sim - ple sweet be - gin - ning, a lov - ing place to start:
3 My hope and ex - pec - ta - tion for true com-mun - i - ty

with Fa - ther, Son, and Spir-it, in wa - ter was re - vealed.
Christ be - gan the sing-ing that swells with-in my heart.
be - gins with res - ur - rec - tion, his death and life in me.

The cleans-ing was for cer - tain, with wa - ter and the Word;
His love be - came my call - ing, his life my min - is - try.
His Spir - it fills the Bod - y: his church through wa - ter sees

gen - tle words were spo - ken, in heav-en they were heard.
His name is my a - dop - tion in - to his fam - i - ly.
prom-ise for to - mor - row, his wa - ter-life in me.

Refrain

They were sing - ing wa - ter - life, be - gin -

ning life, wa - ter - life all my life,

wa-ter - life, Spir - it life, wa-ter - life.

Text: Handt Hanson, b. 1950
Music: WATERLIFE, Handt Hanson
Text and music © 1991 Prince of Peace Publishing, Changing Church, Inc.

Remember and Rejoice

R 162

1 Re - mem - ber and re - joice, re - newed by floods of grace.
2 In life, in death, we trust in God's most ho - ly name,
3 We pledge our - selves a - new to flee the lures of hell,
4 God, bless us by your grace; re - mind us of your care.
5 Re - mem - ber and re - joice, re - newed by floods of grace.

We bear the sign of Je - sus Christ that time can - not e - rase.
for - ev - er traced by wa - ter sign, and sealed by Spir - it - flame.
to cling to Christ's com - mu - ni - ty, in jus - tice, peace to dwell.
Re - new - ing Spir - it, fill us now, in - spire our work, our prayer.
We bear the sign of Je - sus Christ that time can - not e - rase.

Text: Ruth Duck, b. 1947

Music: HEATH   S M, Mason and Webb, *Cantica Lauda*, 1850

R 163

I'm Going on a Journey

1 I'm go-ing on a jour-ney, and I'm start-ing to-day.

My head is wet, and I'm on my way.

God's mark is on me; it's on you, too.

God says he loves me, and he loves you, too!

2 I'm be-com-ing this day   a   saint of God.
3 There are oth - er saints   who have said a-men.

It   real-ly does-n't mat-ter   what   roads I trod.
They'll keep . . me . . faith-ful   to my   jour-ney's end.

Where-ev - er I go   he's been there, too.   God's
A - long . . the way   I   want to be   the

love has touched me   and will car-ry me through.
kind . . of per - son   that . . God . . set free.

Text: Kenneth D. Larkin
Music: WET SAINTS, Edward V. Bonnemère, 1921–1996
Text and music © 1994 Amity Music

R 164

This Is the Spirit's Entry Now

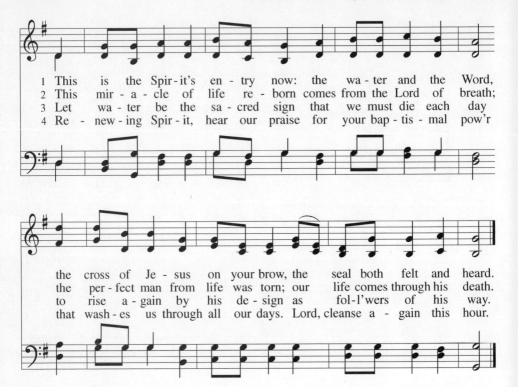

1 This is the Spir-it's en - try now: the wa - ter and the Word,
2 This mir - a - cle of life re - born comes from the Lord of breath;
3 Let wa - ter be the sa - cred sign that we must die each day
4 Re - new - ing Spir - it, hear our praise for your bap - tis - mal pow'r

the cross of Je - sus on your brow, the seal both felt and heard.
the per - fect man from life was torn; our life comes through his death.
to rise a - gain by his de - sign as fol-l'wers of his way.
that wash - es us through all our days. Lord, cleanse a - gain this hour.

Text: Thomas E. Herbranson, b. 1933, alt.
Music: AZMON C M, Carl G. Gläser, 1784–1829
Text © Thomas E. Herbranson

Thy Word

Refrain

Thy word is a lamp un-to my feet and a light un-to my path.

1 When I feel a - fraid, think I've lost my way,
2 I will not for - get your love for me and yet my

still you're there right be - side me, and noth-ing will I fear as
heart for - ev - er is wan - der - ing. Je - sus, be my guide and

Refrain

long as you are near. Please be near me to the end.
hold me to your side, and I will love you to the end.

Text: Amy Grant, b. 1960
Music: THY WORD, Michael W. Smith, b. 1957; arr. Keith Phillips, b. 1957
Text and music © 1984 Word Music, Inc. (ASCAP) and Meadowgreen Music Co./ Bug and Bear Music (ASCAP), admin. EMI Christian Music Publishing

R 166

As Rain from the Clouds

1 As rain from the clouds will your word come to earth,
2 As grain that is scat - tered your word has been sown
3 As rays of the sun shall your word light the world,

as snow from the heav - ens re - fresh - ing the land.
on rocks and on road - ways, in good earth and sand.
a - wak - ing and warm - ing and heal - ing our land.

Then soft - en our soil that the good seed may grow
Make fer - tile our soil that the good seed may grow
Then shine in our hearts that the good seed may grow

and rip - en rich fruit to re - turn to your hand.
and rip - en rich fruit to re - turn to your hand.
and rip - en rich fruit to re - turn to your hand.

We praise you, our God, for the dew of your word;
We praise you, our God, for the seed of your word;
We praise you, our God, for the light of your word;

we thank you, good gar-d'ner, for your ten-der toil.
we thank you, good gar-d'ner, for your ten-der toil.
we thank you, good gar-d'ner, for your ten-der toil.

We bless you, best farm-er, for hun-dred-fold yield,
We bless you, best farm-er, for hun-dred-fold yield,
We bless you, best farm-er, for hun-dred-fold yield,

for har-vest of grace in our once-bar-ren soil.
for har-vest of grace in our once-bar-ren soil.
for har-vest of grace in our once-bar-ren soil.

Text: Delores Dufner OSB, b. 1939
Music: AFTON WATER 11 11 11 11 D, English traditional; arr. Robert Buckley Farlee, b. 1950
Text © 1983, 1998 Sisters of St. Benedict
Arr. © 2003 Augsburg Fortress

R 167

Come, Share the Spirit

1 Come, share the Spir - it, Christ has called us to ven - tures in
2 Come, drown your sins be - neath the wa - ters where life flows from
3 Come, God in - vites us to the ban - quet that ev - 'ry peo -
4 Come, let us tell the gos - pel sto - ry, how God has giv -

the life of faith, to bring good tid - ings to the need - y,
the gran - ite rock, the stone from which our Lord has ris - en,
ple soon will share, with shouts of joy and loud thanks-giv - ing
en us new birth and rais - es us to live for oth - ers,

to tell of vic - t'ry o - ver death. Christ speaks and all
our cor - ner - stone and build - ing block. Christ speaks and rais -
be - fore God's throne we will ap - pear. Christ speaks and bids
to speak good news through-out the earth. Christ speaks and life

of life is new; God's word is pure and it is true.
es from the dead all those who hear the liv - ing word.
us sit and dine; his bod - y, bread, his blood, the wine.
is come a - gain. Good news, good news for ev - 'ry - one!

Text: Gracia Grindal, b. 1943
Music: O DASS ICH TAUSEND ZUNGEN HÄTTE   9 8 9 8 8 8, Johann B. König, 1691–1758
Text © 1987 Augsburg Publishing House

By Your Hand You Feed Your People

R 168

1 By your hand you feed your peo - ple, food of an - gels, heav-en's bread.
2 In this meal we taste your sweet-ness, bread for hun - ger, wine of peace.
3 Send us now with faith and cour-age to the hun - gry, lost, be - reaved.

For these gifts we did not la - bor, by your grace have we been fed:
Ho - ly word and ho - ly wis-dom sat - is - fy our deep-est needs.
In our liv - ing and our dy - ing, we be - come what we re - ceive:

Refrain

Christ's own bod - y, blessed and bro - ken, cup o'er-flow-ing, life out - poured,

giv - en as a liv - ing to - ken of your world re - deemed, re - stored.

Text: Susan R. Briehl, b. 1952
Music: CAMROSE 8 7 8 7 D, Marty Haugen, b. 1950

R 169

Jesus Is Here Right Now

Je - sus is here right now. Je - sus is here.

With this bread and wine true peace you'll find;

Christ Je - sus is here right now.

Text: Leon C. Roberts, 1950–1998

Music: Jesus Is Here, Leon C. Roberts

I Come with Joy

R 170

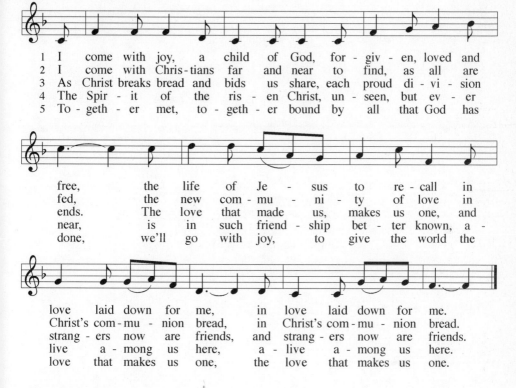

1 I come with joy, a child of God, for - giv - en, loved and
2 I come with Chris - tians far and near to find, as all are
3 As Christ breaks bread and bids us share, each proud di - vi - sion
4 The Spir - it of the ris - en Christ, un - seen, but ev - er
5 To - geth - er met, to - geth - er bound by all that God has

free, the life of Je - sus to re - call in
fed, the new com - mu - ni - ty of love in
ends. The love that made us, makes us one, and
near, is in such friend - ship bet - ter known, a -
done, we'll go with joy, to give the world the

love laid down for me, in love laid down for me.
Christ's com - mu - nion bread, in Christ's com - mu - nion bread.
strang - ers now are friends, and strang - ers now are friends.
live a - mong us here, a - live a - mong us here.
love that makes us one, the love that makes us one.

Text: Brian A. Wren, b. 1936
Music: DOVE OF PEACE 8 6 8 6 6, W. Walker, *Southern Harmony*, 1835
Text © 1971, rev. 1995 Hope Publishing Co. All rights reserved.

R 171

Seed That in Earth Is Dying

1 Seed that in earth is dy - ing grows in - to ears of
2 We were bap - tized in Je - sus, in - to his death and
3 Seed that in earth is dy - ing ris - es to bear much

grain. Grapes that are crushed in the ves - sel
grave, to res - ur - rec - tion's prom - ise:
fruit. Christ, as we meet at your ta - ble,

turn in - to gold - en wine. God, through this mys - ter - y
praise and e - ter - nal life. Heav - en's own prais - es be -
give us the bread of life. Lord, we do thank and a -

grant us faith in our deep - est dark - ness, life in our night and death.
gin here where you your - self are near us, deep in our night and death.
dore you! Un - ceas - ing praise of the a - ges ris - es from night and death.

Text: Harald Herresthal, b. 1944; tr. Hedwig T. Durnbaugh, b. 1929
Music: SÅKORN SOM DØR I JORDEN   7 6 7-6 7 7 6, Harald Herresthal
Music © Norsk Musikforlag A/S
English text © Hedwig T. Durnbaugh

Welcome Table

1 I'm a-goin'-a eat at the wel-come ta - ble,
2 I'm a-goin'-a feast on milk and hon - ey,
3 I'm a-goin'-a wade 'cross Jor - dan's riv - er,

I'm a-goin'-a eat at the wel-come ta-ble, some of these days.
I'm a-goin'-a feast on milk and hon-ey, some of these days.
I'm a-goin'-a wade 'cross Jor - dan's riv-er, some of these days.

I'm a-goin'-a eat at the wel - come ta - ble,
I'm a-goin'-a feast on milk and hon - ey,
I'm a-goin'-a wade 'cross Jor - dan's riv - er,

I'm goin' - a eat at the wel - come ta - ble, some of these days.
I'm goin' - a feast on milk and hon - ey, some of these days.
I'm goin' - a wade 'cross Jor - dan's riv - er, some of these days.

Text: African American spiritual
Music: WELCOME TABLE, African American spiritual; arr. Mark Hayes, b. 1953
Arr. © 2003 Augsburg Fortress

Soul, Adorn Yourself with Gladness

R 173

Vengo a ti, Jesús amado

1 Soul, a- dorn your- self with glad- ness, leave the gloom- y haunts of
2 Has- ten as a bride to meet him, ea- ger- ly and glad- ly
3 Je- sus, source of last- ing pleas- ure, tru- est friend, and dear- est

1 Ven- go a ti, Je- sús a- ma- do: lí- bra- me de mi pe-
2 Vi- da_o- fre- ce, y paz pre- cio- sa tu pa- la- bra po- de-
3 Ya mi al- ma tú li- bras- te, y_el pe- ca- do tú qui-

sad- ness, come in- to the day- light's splen- dor,
greet him. There he stands al- read- y knock- ing;
treas- ure, peace be- yond all un- der- stand- ing,

ca- do. Cal- ma, Re- den- tor, mi llan- to;
ro- sa; por u- nir- se_al e- le- men- to
tas- te, cual pre- lu- dio de tu cie- lo,

there with joy your prais- es ren- der.
quick- ly, now, your gate un- lock- ing,
joy in- to all life ex- pand- ing:

he pe- ca- do tan- to, tan- to.
ha- ce_el san- to sac- ra- men- to.
hoy me go- zo_en tu con- sue- lo.

Bless the one whose grace un- bound- ed this a- maz- ing ban- quet
o- pen wide the fast- closed por- tal, say- ing to the Lord im-
humb- ly now, I bow be- fore you, love in- car- nate, I a-

Con la san- gre que ver- tis- te das con- sue- lo_al al- ma
Con el pan y vi- no_ad- quie- ro cuer- po_y san- gre del Cor-
Cie- los, tie- rra, no- che_y dí- a te den gra- cias a por-

found- ed; he, though heav'n- ly, high, and ho- ly,
mor- tal: "Come, and leave your loved one nev- er;
dore you; worth- i- ly let me re- ceive you,

tris- te; ham- bre tor- nas en har- tu- ra,
de- ro. ¡Oh, mis- te- rio tan pro- fun- do!
fí- a: "Por tus múl- ti- ples fa- vo- res,

deigns to dwell with you most low - ly.
dwell with - in my heart for - ev - er."
and, so fa - vored, nev - er leave you.

sal - va - ción me das se - gu - ra.
¿Quién lo en - tien - de en es - te mun - do?
¡gra - cias mil y mil lo - o - res!"

Refrain/Estribillo

Be thank - ful! Be thank - ful!
¡Oh Cris - to! ¡Oh Cris - to!

Soul, a - dorn your - self with glad - ness, and re - joice!
Ge - ne - ros - o tú me o - fre - ces la sa - lud,

Bless the one whose grace un - bound - ed is our joy.
que a los tu - yos siem - pre das con ple - ni - tud.

Text: Johann Franck, stanzas, 1618–1677; Esther E. Bertieaux, refrain; tr. of stanzas, Albert Lehenbauer, 1891–1955 (Spanish) and *Lutheran Book of Worship*, 1978 (English); tr. of refrain composite

Music: CANTO AL BORINQUEN L M D, Evy Lucío

Spanish stanzas text © 1964 Publicaciones "El Escudo," admin. Augsburg Fortress; Spanish refrain text and English tr. © 1978, 1998 Augsburg Fortress
Music © Peer Music International

R174

Come to the Table

Come to the ta-ble of mer-cy, pre-pared with the wine and the bread.

All who are hun-gry and thirst-y, come and your souls will be fed.

Come at the Lord's in-vi-ta-tion; re-ceive from his nail-scarred hand.

Eat of the bread of sal-va-tion; drink of the blood of the Lamb.

Text: Claire Cloninger, b. 1942

Music: COME TO THE TABLE 8 8 8 7 8 7 8 7, Martin J. Nystrom, b. 1956

Text and music © 1991 Integrity's Hosanna! Music/ASCAP & Juniper Landing Music (admin. Word Music) & Word Music/ASCAP.

United at the Table
Unidos en la fiesta

Refrain / Estribillo

U - nit - ed at the ta - ble: all our joy is
U - ni - dos en la fies - ta, la_a - le - grí - a

joined in song. U - ni - ted in the faith:
se_ha - ce can - ción. U - ni - dos en la fe,

all our joy to God be - longs.
la_a - le - grí - a se_ha - ce_o - ra - ción.

1 We will praise God, we will sing al - le - lu - ias with
2 We will praise God, we will feast at the boun - ti - ful
3 We will praise God, we will play al - le - lu - ias with

1 *Can - ta - re - mos al Se - ñor a - le - lu - yas con*
2 *Can - ta - re - mos la bon - dad del Se - ñor que nos*
3 *Can - ta - re - mos al Se - ñor a - le - lu - yas al*

hymns and with psalm-o - dy; we will praise God for the
ta - ble of life and grace; we will praise God and give
rhy - thm and in - stru - ments; we will praise God for the

him - nos y sal - mos, por - que gran - de_es el a -
sien - ta_a su me - sa, y nos lla - ma_a co - mul -
son de_in - stru - men - tos, y se - rá nues - tra can -

Refrain / Estribillo

love that sus - tains us e - ter - nal - ly.
thanks for com - mu - nion with ev - 'ry race.
love that in - vites all cre - a - tion to dance.

mor que_en no - so - tros por siem - pre mos - tró.
gar co - mo_her - ma - nos su vi - no_y su pan.
ción la_a - la - ban - za que_en - sal - za su_a - mor.

Spanish text: Joaquín Madurga; English text: Angel Mattos, b. 1947, and Gerhard Cartford, b. 1923

Music: UNIDOS EN LA FIESTA 7 10 7 9 and refrain, Joaquín Madurga

Text and music © 1979 J. Madurga and San Pablo Internacional—SSP, admin. OCP Publications, sole U.S. agent. All rights reserved.

R 176

Holy, Holy, Holy
Santo, santo, santo

Ho - ly, ho - ly, ho - ly, my heart, my heart a - dores you!
¡San - to, san - to, san - to. Mi co - ra - zón te_a - do - ra!

My heart is glad to say the words: You are ho - ly, God!
Mi co - ra - zón te sa - be de-cir: ¡San - to e - res Dios!

Text: Argentine traditional
Music: ARGENTINE SANTO, Argéntine traditional

R 177

Bread of Life from Heaven

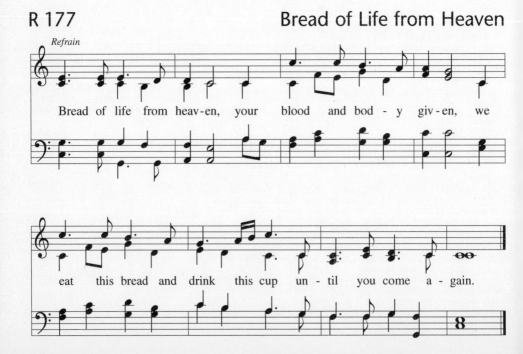

Refrain

Bread of life from heav-en, your blood and bod - y giv-en, we

eat this bread and drink this cup un - til you come a - gain.

1 Break now the bread of Christ's sac - ri - fice; giv - ing
2 Seek not the food that will pass a - way; set your
3 Love as the one who, in love for you, gave him -
4 Take in the light that will nev - er dim, taste the
5 Dwell in the one who now dwells in you; make your
6 Drink of this cup and de - clare his death; eat this

thanks, hun - gry ones, gath - er round.
hearts on the food that en - dures.
self for the life of the world.
life that is strong - er than death.
home in the life - giv - ing Word.
bread and be - lieve Eas - ter morn;

Eat, all of you, and be sat - is - fied; in Christ's
Come, learn the true and the liv - ing way, that the
Come to the one who is food for you, that your
Live in the one who will come and then raise you
Know on - ly Christ, Ho - ly One of God, and be -
trust his re - turn and, with ev - 'ry breath, praise the

Refrain

pres - ence the loaves will a - bound.
full - ness of life may be yours.
hun - ger and thirst be no more.
up at the last with the blest.
lieve in the truth you have heard.
one in whom you are re - born.

Text: Susan R. Briehl, b. 1952
Music: 9 9 9 9 and refrain; Argentine traditional, refrain; Marty Haugen, b. 1950, stanzas

Let Us Go Now to the Banquet
Vamos todos al banquete

Refrain / Estribillo

Let us go now to the ban-quet, to the
Va - mos to - dos al ban - que - te, a la

feast of the u - ni - verse. The ta-ble's set and a place is
me - sa de la crea - ción; ca - da cual con su ta - bu -

wait-ing; come, ev-'ry - one, with your gifts to share.
re - te tie-ne un pues - to y u - na mi - sión.

1 I will rise in the ear - ly morn-ing; the com-
2 God in - vites all the poor and hun - gry to the
3 May we build such a place a - mong us where all

1 Hoy me le - van - to muy tem - pra - no; ya me es-
2 Dios in - vi - ta a to - dos los po - bres a e - sa
3 Dios nos man - da a ha-cer de es - te mun - do u - na

mu - ni - ty's wait - ing for me. With a spring in my step I'm
ban-quet of jus - tice and good where the har - vest will not be
peo - ple are e - qual in love. God has called us to work to -

pe - ra la co - mu - ni - dad; voy su - bien-do a - le - gre la
me - sa co - mún por la fe, don - de no hay a-ca - pa - ra
me - sa don-de ha-ya i-gual-dad, tra - ba - jan-do y lu-chan-do

Refrain / Estribillo

walk - ing with my friends and my fam - i - ly.
hoard-ed so that no one will lack for food.
geth - er and to share ev - ery-thing we have.

cues - ta, voy en bus - ca de tu a - mis - tad.
do - res y a na - die le fal-ta el con - qué.
jun - tos, com - par - tien - do la pro - pie - dad.

Text: Guillermo Cuéllar, b. 1955; tr. Bret Hesla and William Dexheimer-Pharris
Music: VAMOS TODOS AL BANQUETE   9 9 9 8 and refrain, Guillermo Cuéllar

Here, O Lord, Your Servants Gather

R 179

1 Here, O Lord, your ser - vants gath - er, hand we link with hand;
2 Man - y are the tongues we speak, .. scat - tered are the lands,
3 Na - ture's se - crets o - pen wide, .. chang - es nev - er cease.
4 Grant, O God, an age re - newed, filled with death - less love;

look - ing toward our Sav - ior's cross, joined in love we stand.
yet our hearts are one in God, one in love's de - mands.
Where, oh where, can wea - ry souls find the source of peace?
help us as we work and pray; send us from a - bove

As we seek the realm of God, we u - nite to pray:
E'en in dark - ness hope ap - pears, call - ing age and youth:
Un - to all those sore dis - tressed, torn by end - less strife:
truth and cour - age, faith and pow - er, need - ed in our strife:

Je - sus, sav - ior, guide our steps, for you are the way.
Je - sus, teach - er, dwell with us, for you are the truth.
Je - sus, heal - er, bring your balm, for you are the life.
Je - sus, mas - ter, be our way, be our truth, our life.

Text: Tokuo Yamaguchi, b. 1900; tr. Everett M. Stowe, b. 1897

Music: TŌKYŌ, Japanese gagaku mode; arr. Isao Koizumi, 1907–1992

Come and Fill
Confitemini Domino

Ostinato Refrain

Come and fill our hearts with your peace. You a-lone, O Lord, are ho-ly.
Con - fi - te - mi - ni Do - mi - no quo - ni - am bo - nus.

Come and fill our hearts with your peace. Al-le-lu - ia!
Con - fi - te - mi - ni Do - mi - no. Al - le - lu - ia!

Text: Psalm 136:1 (Latin); Taizé Community, 1982

Music: Confitemini Domino, Jacques Berthier, 1923–1994

Text and music © 1982, 1991 Les Presses de Taizé, GIA Publications, Inc., agent

All Who Hunger, Gather Gladly

1 All who hun-ger, gath-er glad-ly; ho-ly man-na is our bread.
2 All who hun-ger, nev-er strang-ers, seek-er, be a wel-come guest.
3 All who hun-ger, sing to-geth-er, Je-sus Christ is liv-ing bread.

Come from wil-der-ness and wan-d'ring. Here in truth we will be fed.
Come from rest-less-ness and roam-ing. Here in joy we keep the feast.
Come from lone-li-ness and long-ing. Here in peace we have been fed.

You that yearn for days of full-ness, all a-round us is our food.
We that once were lost and scat-tered in com-mun-ion's love have stood.
Blest are those who from this ta-ble live their days in grat-i-tude.

Taste and see the grace e-ter-nal. Taste and see that God is good.
Taste and see the grace e-ter-nal. Taste and see that God is good.
Taste and see the grace e-ter-nal. Taste and see that God is good.

Text: Sylvia G. Dunstan, 1955–1993
Music: HOLY MANNA 8 7 8 7 D, W. Moore, *Columbian Harmony*, 1825; arr. Robert Buckley Farlee, b. 1950

R 182

The Trumpets Sound, the Angels Sing

1 The trum-pets sound, the an-gels sing, the feast is
2 Ta-bles are la-den with good things; oh, taste the
3 The hun-gry heart he sat-is-fies, of-fers the

read-y to be-gin. The gates of heav'n are o-pen wide,
peace and joy he brings. He'll fill you up with love di-vine;
poor his par-a-dise. Now hear all heav'n and earth ap-plaud

and Je-sus wel-comes you in-side.
he'll turn your wa-ter in-to wine.
the a-maz-ing good-ness of the Lord.

Refrain

Sing with thank-ful-ness songs of pure de-light. Come and rev-el in

heav-en's love and light. Take your place at the ta-ble of the King.

The feast is read-y to be-gin, the feast is read-y to be-gin.

Text: Graham Kendrick, b. 1950
Music: THE FEAST IS READY   L M and refrain, Graham Kendrick

As We Gather at Your Table

R 183

1 As we gath-er at your ta-ble, as we lis-ten to your word,
2 Turn our wor-ship in-to wit-ness in the sac-ra-ment of life;
3 Gra-cious Spir-it, help us sum-mon o-ther guests to share that feast

help us know, O God, your pres-ence; let our hearts and minds be stirred.
send us forth to love and serve you, bring-ing peace where there is strife.
where tri-um-phant love will wel-come those who had been last and least.

Nour-ish us with sa-cred sto-ry till we claim it as our own;
Give us, Christ, your great com-pas-sion to for-give as you for-gave;
There no more will en-vy blind us nor will pride our peace de-stroy,

teach us through this ho-ly ban-quet how to make Love's vic-t'ry known.
may we still be-hold your im-age in the world you died to save.
as we join with saints and an-gels to re-peat the sound-ing joy.

Text: Carl P. Daw Jr., b. 1944

Music: In Babilone   8 7 8 7 D, Dutch folk tune, 18th cent.; arr. Julius Röntgen, 1855–1932

What Is This Place

1 What is this place where we are meet-ing? On - ly a house, the
2 Words from a - far, stars that are fall - ing, sparks that are sown in
3 And we ac - cept bread at this ta - ble, bro - ken and shared, a

earth its floor. Walls and a roof shel - ter - ing peo - ple,
us like seed: names for our God, dreams, signs and won - ders
liv - ing sign. Here in this world, dy - ing and liv - ing,

win-dows for light, an o - pen door. Yet it be-comes a bod - y that lives
sent from the past are all we need. We in this place re - mem-ber and speak
we are each oth-er's bread and wine. This is the place where we can re-ceive

when we are gath - ered here, and know our God is near.
a - gain what we have heard: God's free re - deem-ing word.
what we need to in - crease: our jus - tice and God's peace.

Text: Huub Oosterhuis, b. 1933; tr. David Smith, b. 1933
Music: KOMT NU MET ZANG 9 8 9 8 9 6 6, A. Valerius' *Nederlandtsch Gedenckclanck,* 1626; arr. Adrian Engels, b. 1906
Tr. and arr. © 1967 Gooi en Sticht, BV, Baarn, The Netherlands. All rights reserved. OCP Publications, exclusive agent for English-language countries.

You Are Holy

You are ho - ly, you are whole. You are al - ways ev - er more
than we ev - er un - der - stand. You are al - ways at hand.
Bless - ed are you com - ing near. Bless - ed are you com - ing here
to your church in wine and bread, raised from soil, raised from dead.
You are ho - ly, you are whole - ness, you are pres - ent.
Let the cos - mos praise you, Lord! Sing ho - san - na in the
high - est! Sing ho - san - na! Sing ho - san - na to our God!

Text: Per Harling, b. 1945

Music: Du är helig, Per Harling

Text and music © 1990 Ton Vis Produktion AB, admin. Augsburg Fortress in North America, South America, and Central America, including the Caribbean.

R 186

God Be with You Till We Meet Again

1 God be with you till we meet a - gain; by his
2 God be with you till we meet a - gain; 'neath his
3 God be with you till we meet a - gain; when life's
4 God be with you till we meet a - gain; keep love's

coun - sels guide, up - hold you, with his sheep se - cure - ly
wings se - cure - ly hide you, dai - ly man - na still pro -
per - ils thick con - found you, put his arms un - fail - ing
ban - ner float - ing o'er you, smite death's threat - 'ning wave be -

fold you;
vide you;
'round you;   God be with you till we meet a - gain.
fore you;

Refrain

Till we meet, till we meet, till we meet at Je - sus' feet;

till we meet, till we meet a - gain, till we meet,

till we meet, till we meet, God be with you till we meet a - gain.

till we meet, till we meet a - gain,

Text: Jeremiah E. Rankin, 1828–1904
Music: GOD BE WITH YOU   9 8 8 9 and refrain, William G. Tomer, 1833–1896

Go, Make Disciples

Go, make dis - ci - ples, bap - tiz - ing them,

teach - ing them. Go, make dis - ci - ples, for

I am with you till the end of time. Go, be the

salt of the earth. Go, be the light for the world.

Go, be a cit - y on a hill, so all can see that you're

serv - ing me. Go, make dis - ci - ples.

Text: Handt Hanson, b. 1950
Music: GO, MAKE DISCIPLES, Handt Hanson
Text and music © 1996 Prince of Peace Publishing, Changing Church, Inc.

R 188

The Trees of the Field

You shall go out with joy and be led forth with peace, and the
moun-tains and the hills will break forth be - fore you. There'll be
shouts of joy and all the trees of the field will clap, will clap their hands.
And all the trees of the field will clap their hands. The
trees of the field will clap their hands. The trees of the field will
clap their hands, while you go out with joy.

Text: Steffi Geiser Rubin, b. 1950
Music: THE TREES OF THE FIELD, Stuart Dauermann, b. 1944
Text and music © 1975 Lillenas Publishing Company, admin. The Copyright Company. All rights reserved. International copyright secured.

R 189

The Lord Now Sends Us Forth
Enviado soy de Dios

The Lord now sends us forth with hands to serve and give, to
En - via - do soy de Dios, mi ma - no lis - ta es - tá pa -

make of all the earth a bet - ter place to live.
ra cons - truir con él un mun - do fra - ter - nal.

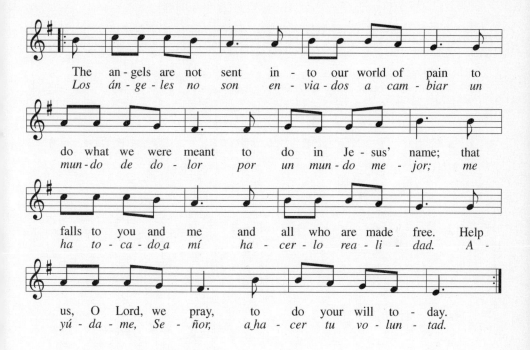

The an-gels are not sent in-to our world of pain to
Los án-ge-les no son en-via-dos a cam-biar un

do what we were meant to do in Je-sus' name; that
mun-do de do-lor por un mun-do me-jor; me

falls to you and me and all who are made free. Help
ha to-ca-do a mí ha-cer-lo rea-li-dad. A-

us, O Lord, we pray, to do your will to-day.
yú-da-me, Se-ñor, a ha-cer tu vo-lun-tad.

Text: Central American anonymous; tr. Gerhard Cartford, b. 1923
Music: ENVIADO   13 13 13 12 12 12, Central American anonymous
Tr. © 1998 Augsburg Fortress

Send Me, Jesus   R 190
Thuma mina

1 Send me, Je-sus;   send me, Je-sus;   send me, Je-sus; send me, Lord.
2 I   am will-ing;   I   am will-ing;   I   am will-ing, will-ing, Lord.
1 Thu-ma mi-na,   thu-ma mi-na,   thu-ma mi-na, Nko-si yam.
2 Ndi-ya vu-ma,   ndi-ya vu-ma,   ndi-ya vu-ma, Nko-si yam.

Send me, Je-sus.

Text: South African traditional
Music: THUMA MINA, NKOSI YAM 4 4 7, South African traditional

R 191

Rise, O Church, like Christ Arisen

1 Rise, O church, like Christ a - ris - en, from this meal of
2 Rise, trans-formed, and choose to fol - low af - ter Christ, though
3 Rise, re - mem - ber well the fu - ture God has called us
4 Ser - vice be our sure vo - ca - tion; cour - age be our

love and grace; may we through such love en - vi - sion
wound-ed, whole; bro - ken, shared, our lives are hal - lowed
to re - ceive; pres - ent by God's lov - ing nur - ture,
dai - ly breath; mer - cy be our des - ti - na - tion

whose we are, and whose, our praise. Al - le - lu - ia,
to re - lease and to con - sole. Al - le - lu - ia,
Spir - it - ed then let us live. Al - le - lu - ia,
from this day and un - to death. Al - le - lu - ia,

al - le - lu - ia: God, the won - der of our days.
al - le - lu - ia: Christ, our pres - ent, past, and goal.
al - le - lu - ia: Spir - it, grace by whom we live.
al - le - lu - ia: Rise, O church, a liv - ing faith.

Text: Susan Palo Cherwien, b. 1953
Music: PRAISE, MY SOUL   8 7 8 7 8 7, John Goss, 1800–1880
Text © 1997 Susan Palo Cherwien, admin. Augsburg Fortress

Praise to the Lord

1 Praise to the Lord, all of you, God's
2 There is none like our God in the heav'ns or on
1 *Lou - ez l'E - ter - nel, ser - vi - teurs de*
2 *Qui est comme no - tre Dieu, dans les cieux, sur la*

ser - vants. Bless - ed be the name of our God
earth, who lifts the poor from the dust, seat - ing them
Dieu. Bé - ni soit son nom, main - te - nant,
ter - re, qui ex - al - te les pauvres au rang des grands

now and ev - er. From the ris - ing of the sun
with the might - y, who stoops to raise the weak and low:
à ja - mais. Du le - ver du so - leil,
de son peu - ple, qui ma - ni - feste mi - sé - ri - corde?

Refrain

may the Lord be praised, praise to the name of the Lord!
bé - ni soit son nom! Lou - é soit Dieu, l'E - ter - nel!

Text: Ron Klusmeier, b. 1946; French tr. R. Gerald Hobbs, b. 1941
Music: RICHARDSON-BURTON, Ron Klusmeier
Text and music © 1972 Ron Klusmeier, 1997 Musiklus

R 193

Joyous Light of Heavenly Glory

1 Joy-ous light of heav'n-ly glo - ry, lov-ing glow of God's own face,
2 In the stars that grace the dark - ness, in the blaz-ing sun of dawn,
3 You who made the heav-en's splen-dor, ev-'ry danc-ing star of night,

you who sing cre - a-tion's sto - ry, shine on ev - 'ry land and race.
in the light of peace and wis-dom, we can hear your qui - et song.
make us shine with gen - tle jus - tice, let us each re - flect your light.

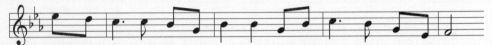

Now as eve - ning falls a - round us, we shall raise our songs to you.
Love that fills the night with won-der, love that warms the wea - ry soul,
Might-y God of all cre - a - tion, gen - tle Christ who lights our way,

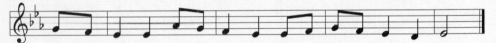

God of day-break, God of shad-ows, come and light our hearts a - new.
love that bursts all chains a.- sun - der, set us free and make us whole.
lov - ing Spir - it of sal - va - tion, lead us on to end - less day.

Text: Marty Haugen, b. 1950
Music: JOYOUS LIGHT 8 7 8 7 D, Marty Haugen
Text and music © 1987 GIA Publications, Inc. All rights reserved.

Now It Is Evening

R194

1 Now it is eve-ning: lights of the cit-y bid us re-
2 Now it is eve-ning; food on the ta-ble bids us re-
3 Now it is eve-ning; lit-tle ones sleep-ing bid us re-
4 Now it is eve-ning; here in our meet-ing may we re-

mem-ber Christ is our light. Man-y are lone-ly, who will be
mem-ber Christ is our life. Man-y are hun-gry, who will be
mem-ber Christ is our peace. Some are ne-glect-ed, who will be
mem-ber Christ is our friend. Some may be strang-ers, who will be

neigh-bor? Where there is car-ing Christ is our light.
neigh-bor? Where there is shar-ing Christ is our life.
neigh-bor? Where there is car-ing Christ is our peace.
neigh-bor? Where there's a wel-come Christ is our friend.

Text: Fred Pratt Green, 1903–2000

Music: BOZEMAN 5 5 5 4 D, Rusty Edwards, b. 1955

R 195

Lord, Support Us All Day Long

1 Lord, sup-port us all day long, guide and strength-en.
2 Be our light in dark-ness, Lord, our de-fend-er;
3 With your pres-ence, Lord, draw near those who la-bor
4 Gra-cious Lord, we give you thanks, praise and bless you,

Eve-ning comes, the world is hushed, shad-ows length-en.
in your pres-ence per-ils all must sur-rend-er.
through the night-time on be-half of their neigh-bor;
as the giv-er of all good we con-fess you;

Work is done, life's fe-vered pace now has end-ed;
Drive a-way sa-tan-ic snares from each dwell-ing;
grant them cour-age for each fear, faith-ful car-ing;
this past day we now com-mit to your keep-ing

Christ, to you, our fi-nal rest is com-mend-ed.
then, at peace, our hearts your praise will be tell-ing.
your com-pas-sion and your love tru-ly shar-ing.
and en-trust to you the hours of our sleep-ing.

Text: Stephen P. Starke, b. 1955
Music: JESU MEINES HERZENS FREUD 7 4 7 4 7 4 7 4, Johann Ahle, 1625–1673; fig. bass Johann Sebastian Bach, 1685–1750; arr. Frank W. Stoldt, b. 1958
Text © 1998 Stephen P. Starke. Arr. © 2003 Augsburg Fortress

My Heart Sings Out with Joyful Praise

R 196

1 My heart sings out with joy-ful praise to God who rais-es me,
2 The arm of God is strong and just to scat-ter all the proud.
3 The prom-ise made in a-ges past at last has come to be,

who came to me when I was low and changed my des-ti-ny.
The ty-rants tum-ble from their thrones and van-ish like a cloud.
for God has come in power to save, to set all peo-ple free.

The Ho-ly One, the liv-ing God, is al-ways full of grace
The hun-gry all are sat-is-fied: the rich are sent a-way.
Re-mem-b'ring those who wait to see sal-va-tion's dawn-ing day,

to those who seek their mak-er's will in ev-'ry time and place.
The poor of earth who suf-fer long will wel-come God's new day.
our Sav-ior comes to all who weep to wipe their tears a-way.

Text: Ruth Duck, b. 1947
Music: MARIAS LOVSÅNG L M D, Swedish folk melody

R 197

We Come to You for Healing, Lord

1 We come to you for heal - ing, Lord, of
2 As once you walked through an - cient streets and
3 You touch us through phy - si - cians' skills, through
4 Through nights of pain and wake - ful - ness, through
5 We come to you, O lov - ing Lord, in

bod - y, mind and soul, and pray that by your
reached toward those in pain, we know you come a -
nurs - es' gifts of care, and through the love of
days when strength runs low, grant us your gift of
our dis - tress and pain, in trust that through our

Spir - it's touch our lives may be made whole.
mong us still with pow'r to heal a - gain.
faith - ful friends who lift our lives in prayer.
pa - tience, Lord, your calm - ing peace to know.
nights and days your grace will heal, sus - tain.

Text: Herman G. Stuempfle Jr., b. 1923
Music: MARTYRDOM   C M, Hugh Wilson, 1766–1824

For by Grace You Have Been Saved

R 198

1. For by grace you have been saved and e - ven faith is not your
2. "So my grace is all - suf - fi - cient for each child who is my
3. So this weak - ness with con - tent - ment I'll ac - cept now in my -

own, it's the gift of God for you and not the
own, for my strength is now made per - fect for each
self, all my hard - ships, pains, and griefs that still lie

works that you have done. Don't let an - y - bod - y
child who is my own. When you're weak, then you are
deep with - in my - self. When I'm weak, then I am

boast, for this is God's great gift. A -
strong, for this is God's great gift." A -
strong, for this is God's great gift. A -

1–2

men.
men.

3

men. A - men.

Text: Kari Tikka, b. 1946; tr. Michael Harper
Music: ARMONLAULU 15 15 15, Kari Tikka
Text and music © Fennica Gehrman, admin. Boosey & Hawkes, Inc.

R 199

Give Me a Clean Heart

Give me a clean heart so I may serve thee.

Lord, fix my heart so that I may be used by thee.

For I'm not wor - thy of all these bless - ings.

Give me a clean heart and I'll fol - low thee.

1 I'm not ask-ing for the rich-es of the land.
2 Some-times I am up and some-times I am down.

I'm not ask-ing for the proud to know my name.
Some-times I am al-most lev-el to the ground.

Please give me, Lord, a clean heart, that I may fol-low thee.
Please give me, Lord, a clean heart, that I may fol-low thee.

Give me a clean heart, a clean heart and I will fol-low thee.
Give me a clean heart, a clean heart and I will fol-low thee.

Text: Margaret J. Douroux, b. 1941
Music: A CLEAN HEART, Margaret J. Douroux
Text and music © 1970 Margaret J. Douroux

R 200

Come, Ye Disconsolate

1 Come, ye dis - con - so - late, wher - e'er ye lan - guish;
2 Joy of the des - o - late, light of the stray - ing,
3 Here see the Bread of life; see wa - ters flow - ing

come to the mer - cy - seat, fer - vent - ly kneel.
hope of the pen - i - tent, fade - less and pure;
forth from the throne of God, pure from a - bove.

Here bring your wound - ed hearts, here tell your an - guish;
here speaks the Com - fort - er, ten - der - ly say - ing,
Come to the feast of love; come, ev - er know - ing

earth has no sor - row that heav'n can - not heal.
"Earth has no sor - row that heav'n can - not cure."
earth has no sor - row but heav'n can re - move.

Text: Thomas Moore, 1779–1852; Thomas Hastings, 1784–1872
Music: CONSOLATOR   11 10 11 10, Samuel Webbe, 1740–1816

Holy God, Holy and Glorious

R 201

1 Ho - ly God, ho - ly and glo - ri - ous,
2 Ho - ly God, ho - ly and pow - er - ful,
3 Ho - ly God, ho - ly and beau - ti - ful,
4 Ho - ly God, ho - ly and on - ly wise,
5 Ho - ly God, ho - ly and liv - ing one,

glo - ry most sub - lime, you come as one a - mong us
pow - er with - out peer, you bend to us in weak - ness;
beau - ty un - sur - passed, you are de - spised, re - ject - ed;
wis - dom of great price, you choose the way of fol - ly:
life that nev - er ends, you show your love by dy - ing,

in - to hu - man time, and we be - hold your glo - ry.
emp - tied, you draw near, and we be - hold your pow - er.
scorned, you hold us fast, and we be - hold your beau - ty.
God the cru - ci - fied, yet we be - hold your wis - dom.
dy - ing for your friends, and we be - hold you liv - ing.

Text: Susan R. Briehl, b. 1952
Music: NELSON 9 5 7 5 7, Robert Buckley Farlee, b. 1950
Text © 2000 GIA Publications, Inc. All rights reserved.
Music © 2001 Robert Buckley Farlee, admin. Augsburg Fortress

R 202

Neither Death nor Life

Refrain

Nei-ther death, nor life, nor an-gels, nor rul-ers, nor trials in the pres-ent, nor an-y trial to come, nei-ther height, nor depth, nor all of cre-a-tion can ev-er sep-a-rate us from the love of God poured out in Christ Je-sus, our Lord.

Leader or All

1 Dwell in the One who raised Christ from the dead; though your

2 All who are led by the Spir-it shall live as

3 All of the suf-f'ring we now must en-dure is

4 All of cre-a-tion a-waits the new birth, the

5 Who can sep-a-rate us from the love of Christ? Will

bod - y   shall   die,   in   Christ   you   shall

chil - dren   of   God,   and   heirs   with   Christ

noth - ing   to   the   glo - ry   so   soon   to   be   re -

full - ness   of   re - demp - tion,   through   la - bor   pains   of

hard - ship   or   dis - tress,   per - se - cu - tion   or

Refrain

rise   through   the   Spir - it   who   brings   you   to   life.

Refrain

Je - sus,   God's   a - dopt - ed   and   cho - sen   and   loved.

Refrain

vealed   when   cre - a - tion   it - self   is   set   free.

Refrain

love,   and   so   we   wait   in   pa - tience   and   hope.

Refrain

fam - ine,   or   na - ked - ness   or   per - il   or   sword?

Text: Marty Haugen, b. 1950
Music: Neither Death nor Life, Marty Haugen

R 203   May Angels Lead with Gentle Hand

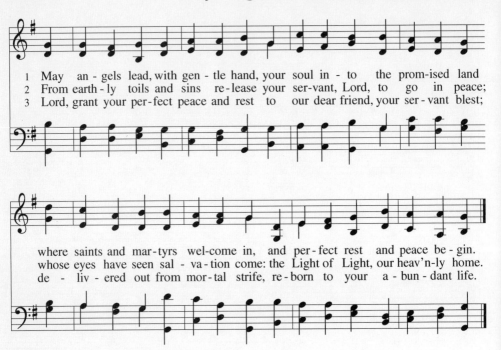

1 May an-gels lead, with gen-tle hand, your soul in-to the prom-ised land
2 From earth-ly toils and sins re-lease your ser-vant, Lord, to go in peace;
3 Lord, grant your per-fect peace and rest to our dear friend, your ser-vant blest;

where saints and mar-tyrs wel-come in, and per-fect rest and peace be-gin.
whose eyes have seen sal-va-tion come: the Light of Light, our heav'n-ly home.
de - liv-ered out from mor-tal strife, re-born to your a-bun-dant life.

Text: Thomas Pavlechko, b. 1962

Music: TALLIS' CANON   L M, Thomas Tallis, 1505–1585

In Our Day of Thanksgiving

R 204

1 In our day of thanks-giv-ing one psalm let us of-fer
2 In the morn-ing of life, and at noon, and at eve-ning,
3 These stones that have ech-oed their prais-es are ho-ly,
4 Sing praise, then, and thanks that God's love here has found them

for the saints who be-fore us have found their re-ward;
they were gath-ered to heav'n from our wor-ship be-low;
and dear is the ground where their feet have once trod;
whose jour-ney is end-ed, whose per-ils are past;

when the shad-ow of death fell up-on them, we sor-rowed,
but not till God's love, at the font and the al-tar,
yet here they con-fessed they were strang-ers and pil-grims,
they be-lieved in the light; and its glo-ry is round them,

but now we re-joice that they rest in the Lord.
had clothed them with grace for the way they should go.
and still they were seek-ing the cit-y of God.
where the clouds of earth's sor-row are lift-ed at last.

Text: William Henry Draper, 1855–1933
Music: St. Catherine's Court 12 11 12 11, Richard Strutt, 1848–1927

When We Are Living
Pues si vivimos

1 When we are liv - ing, it is in Christ Je - sus,
2 'Mid times of sor - row and in times of pain,
3 A - cross this wide world, we shall al - ways find

1 *Pues si vi - vi - mos, pa - ra él vi - vi - mos,*
2 *En la tris - te - za y en el do - lor,*
3 *En es - te mun - do por do-qui - er ha - brá*

and when we're dy - ing, it is in the Lord.
when sens-ing beau - ty or in love's em - brace,
those who are cry - ing with no peace of mind;

y si mo - ri - mos pa - ra él mo - ri - mos.
en la be - lle - za y en el a - mor,
gen - te que llo - ra y sin con - so - lar.

Both in our liv - ing and in our dy - ing,
wheth-er we suf - fer, or sing re - joic - ing,
and when we help them, or when we feed them,

Sea que vi - va - mos o que mu - ra - mos,
sea que su - fra - mos o que go - ce - mos,
Sea que_a - yu - de - mos o_a - li - men - te - mos,

we be - long to God, we be - long to God.
we be - long to God, we be - long to God.
we be - long to God, we be - long to God.

so - mos del Se - ñor, so - mos del Se - ñor.
so - mos del Se - ñor, so - mos del Se - ñor.
so - mos del Se - ñor, so - mos del Se - ñor.

Text: Roberto Escamilla, b. 1931; tr. Elise S. Eslinger, b. 1942, and George Lockwood, b. 1946

Music: SOMOS DEL SEÑOR, Spanish traditional

Spanish text, stanzas 2–4 © 1983 Abingdon Press, admin. Copyright Company; tr. © 1989 The United Methodist Publishing House, admin. Copyright Company.

Lord, It Belongs Not to My Care

R 206

1 Lord, it be - longs not to my care
2 Christ leads me through no dark - er rooms
3 Then shall I end my sad com - plaints

wheth-er I die or live; to love and serve thee
than he went through be - fore; they that un - to God's
and wea - ry, sin - ful days, and join with the tri -

is my share, and this thy grace must give. If
king - dom come must en - ter by this door. Come,
um - phant saints who sing my Sav - ior's praise. My

life be long, I will be glad that I may long o -
Lord, when grace has made me meet thy bless - ed face to
knowl-edge of that life is small, the eye of faith is

bey; if short, yet why should I be sad to
see; for if thy work on earth be sweet, what
dim; but 'tis e - nough that Christ knows all, and

soar to end - less day?
will thy glo - ry be!
I shall be with him.

Text: Richard Baxter, 1615–1691
Music: BAXTER C M D, Carl F. Schalk, b. 1929
Music © 1978 Augsburg Publishing House

R 207

I Heard the Voice of Jesus Say

1 I heard the voice of Je-sus say, "Come un-to me and rest;
2 I heard the voice of Je-sus say, "Be-hold, I free-ly give
3 I heard the voice of Je-sus say, "I am this dark world's light;

lay down, O wea-ry one, lay down your head up-on my breast."
the liv-ing wa-ter, thirst-y one; stoop down and drink and live."
look un-to me, your morn shall rise, and all your day be bright."

I came to Je-sus as I was, so wea-ry, worn, and sad;
I came to Je-sus, and I drank of that life-giv-ing stream;
I looked to Je-sus, and I found in him my star, my sun;

I found in him a rest-ing place, and he has made me glad.
my thirst was quenched, my soul re-vived, and now I live in him.
and in that light of life I'll walk till trav-'ling days are done.

Text: Horatius Bonar, 1808–1889

Music: KINGSFOLD C M D, English traditional; arr. Ralph Vaughan Williams, 1872–1958

On Jordan's Stormy Banks

R 208

1 On Jor-dan's storm-y banks I stand, and cast a wish-ful eye
2 All o'er those wide ex-tend-ed plains shines one e-ter-nal day;
3 No chill-ing winds or poi-s'nous breath can reach that health-ful shore;
4 When shall I reach that hap-py place, and be for-ev-er blest?

to Ca-naan's fair and hap-py land, where my pos-ses-sions lie.
there God the Son for-ev-er reigns and scat-ters night a-way.
sick-ness and sor-row, pain and death, are felt and feared no more.
When shall I see my Sav-ior's face, and in God's bo-som rest?

Refrain

I am bound for the prom-ised land, I am bound for the prom-ised land;

oh, who will come and go with me? I am bound for the prom-ised land.

Text: Samuel Stennett, 1727–1795
Music: PROMISED LAND 8 6 8 6 and refrain, North American traditional; adapt. Rigdon M. McIntosh, 1836–1899

R 209

Deep River

Refrain

Deep riv-er, my home is o-ver Jor-dan,

deep riv-er, Lord, I want to cross o-ver in-to camp-ground.

1 Oh, don't you want to go to that gos - pel feast, that
2 Oh, when I get to heav-en, I'll take my seat, and

prom - ised land where all is peace? Oh,
cast my crown at Je - sus' feet. Oh,

Refrain

Text: African American spiritual
Music: DEEP RIVER, African American spiritual

When Peace, like a River

It Is Well

1. When peace, like a riv-er, at-tend-eth my way; when
sor-rows, like sea bil-lows, roll; what-ev-er my lot, thou hast
taught me to say, it is well, it is well with my soul.

2. Though Sa-tan should buf-fet, though tri-als should come, let
this blest as-sur-ance con-trol, that Christ hath re-gard-ed my
help-less es-tate, and hath shed his own blood for my soul.

3. He lives—oh, the bliss of this glo-ri-ous thought; my
sin, not in part, but the whole, is nailed to his cross and I
bear it no more. Praise the Lord, praise the Lord, O my soul!

4. And Lord, haste the day when our faith shall be sight, the
clouds be rolled back as a scroll, the trum-pet shall sound and the
Lord shall de-scend; e-ven so it is well with my soul.

Refrain

It is well with my soul, it is well, it is well with my soul.

it is well with my soul,

Text: Horatio G. Spafford, 1828–1888
Music: VILLE DU HAVRE   11 8 11 9, Philip P. Bliss, 1838–1876

R 211

Sing of the Lord's Goodness

1 Sing of the Lord's good-ness, Fa-ther of all wis-dom,
2 Pow-er he has wield-ed, hon-or is his gar-ment,
3 Cour-age in our dark-ness, com-fort in our sor-row,
4 Praise him with your sing-ing, praise him with the trum-pet,

come to him and bless his name. Mer-cy he has shown us,
ris-en from the snares of death. His word he has spo-ken,
Spir-it of our God most high; so-lace for the wea-ry,
praise him with the lute and harp; praise him with the cym-bals,

his love is for-ev-er, faith-ful to the end of days.
one bread he has bro-ken, new life he now gives to all.
par-don for the sin-ner, splen-dor of the liv-ing God.
praise him with your danc-ing, praise God till the end of days.

Refrain

Come then, all you na-tions, sing of the Lord's good-ness,

mel-o-dies of praise and thanks to God.

Ring out the Lord's glo-ry, praise him with your mu-sic,

wor-ship him and bless his name.

Text: Ernest Sands, b. 1949
Music: THE LORD'S GOODNESS 6 6 7 6 6 7 and refrain, Ernest Sands
Text and music © 1981 Ernest Sands

Behold, How Pleasant
Miren qué bueno

Refrain / Estribillo

Be - hold, how plea - sant, how good it is!
Mir - en qué bue - no qué bue - no es.

1 How plea-sant and har - mon - ious when God's peo-ple are to - geth - er:
2 How plea-sant and har - mon - ious when God's peo-ple are to - geth - er:
3 How plea-sant and har - mon - ious when God's peo-ple are to - geth - er:

1 *Mir - en qué bue-no es cuan-do to - do el pue-blo es - tá jun - to.*
2 *Mir - en qué bue-no es cuan-do to - do el pue-blo es - tá jun - to:*
3 *Mir - en qué bue-no es cuan-do to - do el pue-blo es - tá jun - to:*

Refrain / Estribillo

fra - grant as pre - cious oil when run - ning fresh on Aa - ron's beard.
re - fresh - ing as the dew up - on the moun-tain of the Lord.
there the Lord God be - stows a bless-ing— life for - ev - er - more.

Es co - mo a - cei - te bue - no de - rra - ma - do so - bre Aa-rón.
se pa - ra - ce al ro - cío o so - bre los mon-tes de Síon.
por - que el Se - ñor ahi man - da vi - da e - ter - na y ben - di - ción.

Text: Pablo Sosa, b. 1933, based on Psalm 133
Music: MIREN QUÉ BUENO, Pablo Sosa
Text and music © Pablo Sosa

R 213 Although I Speak with Angel's Tongue

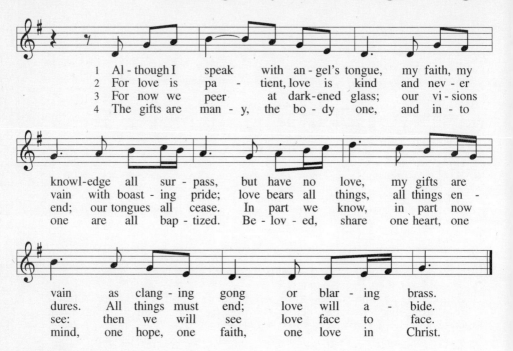

1. Al - though I speak with an - gel's tongue, my faith, my
2. For love is pa - tient, love is kind and nev - er
3. For now we peer at dark-ened glass; our vi - sions
4. The gifts are man - y, the bo - dy one, and in - to

knowl-edge all sur - pass, but have no love, my gifts are
vain with boast - ing pride; love bears all things, all things en -
end; our tongues all cease. In part we know, in part now
one are all bap - tized. Be - lov - ed, share one heart, one

vain as clang - ing gong or blar - ing brass.
dures. All things must end; love will a - bide.
see: then we will see love face to face.
mind, one hope, one faith, one love in Christ.

Text: Andrew Donaldson, b. 1951, based on 1 Corinthians 13
Music: O WALY WALY   L M, English traditional
Text © 1995 Andrew Donaldson

R 214 Stand in the Congregation

1. I will stand in the con - gre - ga - tion and I will ex -
2. I will stand in the con - gre - ga - tion and I will
3. We will join as a con - gre - ga - tion and we will ex -

alt you; I will stand in the con - gre - ga -
praise your name; I will stand in the con - gre - ga -
alt you; we will join as a con - gre - ga -

- tion and I will ex - alt you. Let the
- tion and I will praise your name. With your
- tion and we will ex - alt you. We will

chil-dren of your sal - va - tion lift their prais - es too!
peo - ple in ev - 'ry na - tion I will shout this praise!
sing as all cre - a - tion lifts the song a - new!

1, 2

Hal - le - lu - jah!

3

Hal - le - lu - jah! Hal - le - lu - jah!

Hal - le - lu - jah! Hal - le - lu - jah!

Let the chil - dren of your sal - va - tion lift their

prais - es too! Hal - le - lu - jah!

Text: Bill Batstone

Music: STAND IN THE CONGREGATION, Bill Batstone

Text and music © 1988 Maranatha Praise, Inc., admin. The Copyright Company. All rights reserved. International copyright secured.

Where True Charity and Love Abide

Ubi caritas et amor

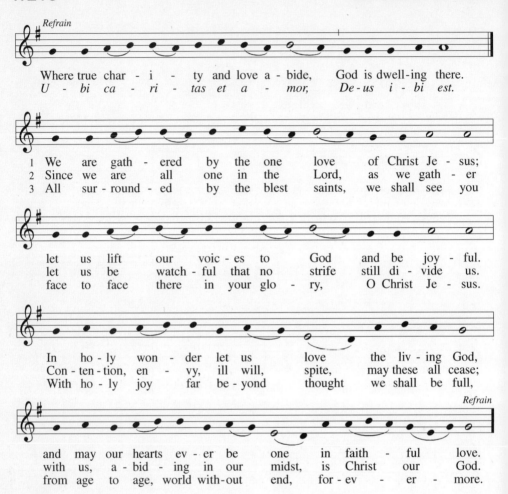

Refrain

Where true char - i - ty and love a - bide, God is dwell-ing there.
U - bi ca - ri - tas et a - mor, De-us i - bi est.

1 We are gath - ered by the one love of Christ Je - sus;
2 Since we are all one in the Lord, as we gath - er
3 All sur - round - ed by the blest saints, we shall see you

let us lift our voic - es to God and be joy - ful.
let us be watch - ful that no strife still di - vide us.
face to face there in your glo - ry, O Christ Je - sus.

In ho - ly won - der let us love the liv - ing God,
Con - ten - tion, en - vy, ill will, spite, may these all cease;
With ho - ly joy far be - yond thought we shall be full,

Refrain

and may our hearts ev - er be one in faith - ful love.
with us, a - bid - ing in our midst, is Christ our God.
from age to age, world with-out end, for - ev - er - more.

Text: Latin, 9th cent.; tr. composite
Music: UBI CARITAS, plainsong, mode 6
Text © 1995, 2001 Augsburg Fortress

Bring Many Names

R 216

1 Bring man - y names, beau - ti - ful and good,
2 Strong moth - er God, work - ing night and day,
3 Warm fa - ther God, hug - ging ev - 'ry child,
4 Old, ach - ing God, gray with end - less care,
5 Young, grow - ing God, ea - ger, on the move,
6 Great, liv - ing God, nev - er ful - ly known,

cel - e - brate, in par - a - ble and sto - ry, ho - li - ness in
plan - ning all the won - ders of cre - a - tion, set - ting each e -
feel - ing all the strains of hu - man liv - ing, car - ing and for -
calm - ly pierc-ing e - vil's new dis - guis - es, glad of good sur -
say - ing no to false-hood and un - kind - ness, cry - ing out for
joy - ful dark-ness far be - yond our see - ing, clos - er yet than

glo - ry, liv - ing, lov - ing God. Hail and ho -
qua - tion, gen - i - us at play: Hail and ho -
giv - ing till we're rec - on - ciled: Hail and ho -
pris - es, wis - er than de - spair: Hail and ho -
jus - tice, giv - ing all you have: Hail and ho -
breath - ing, ev - er - last - ing home: Hail and ho -

1–5

san - na! Bring man - y names!
san - na, strong moth - er God!
san - na, warm fa - ther God!
san - na, old, ach - ing God!
san - na, young, grow - ing God!

6

san - na, great, liv - ing God!

Text: Brian A. Wren, b. 1936

Music: WESTCHASE 9 10 11 9, Carlton R. Young, b. 1926

We Are All One in Christ
Somos uno

R 217

We are all one in Christ, we are one bod - y, all one peo - ple out of man - y. man - y.
So - mos u - no en Cris - to, so - mos u - no. So - mos u - no, u - no so - lo. so - lo.

There is one God, and on - ly one Lord; there is one faith, one ho - ly love. There is one bap - tism; there is one Spir - it, who is God the com - fort - er.
Un so - lo Dios, un so - lo Se - ñor, u - na so - la fe, un so - lo a - mor. Un so - lo bau - tis - mo, un so - lo Es - pí - ri - tu, y e - se es el con - so - la - dor.

Text: anonymous; tr. Gerhard Cartford, b. 1923
Music: SOMOS UNO, anonymous
Tr. © 1998 Augsburg Fortress

Beloved, God's Chosen

R 218

1 Be - lov - ed, God's cho - sen, put on as a gar - ment
2 With - in, call forth Wis - dom, to dwell in you rich - ly;
3 Be - lov - ed, God's cho - sen, put on as a gar - ment

com - pas - sion, for - give - ness, and good - ness of heart.
let peace rule your hearts and that peace be of Christ.
com - pas - sion, for - give - ness, and good - ness of heart.

A - bove all, be - fore all, let love be your rai - ment
And from the heart's cham - ber, be - lov - ed and ho - ly,
A - bove all, be - fore all, let love be your rai - ment

that binds in - to one ev - 'ry dis - so - nant part.
let sing - ing thanks - giv - ing to God ev - er rise.
that binds in - to one ev - 'ry dis - so - nant part.

Text: Susan Palo Cherwien, b. 1953
Music: ST. CATHERINE'S COURT   12 11 12 11, Richard Strutt, 1848–1927
Text © 1994 Susan Palo Cherwien, admin. Augsburg Fortress

R 219

All Are Welcome

1 Let us build a house where love can dwell and all can safe - ly live, a place where saints and chil - dren tell how hearts learn to for - give. Built of hopes and dreams and vi - sions, rock of faith and vault of grace; here the love of Christ shall end di - vi - sions:

2 Let us build a house where proph - ets speak, and words are strong and true, where all God's chil - dren dare to seek to dream God's reign a - new. Here the cross shall stand as wit - ness and as sym - bol of God's grace; here as one we claim the faith of Je - sus:

3 Let us build a house where love is found in wa - ter, wine and wheat: a ban - quet hall on ho - ly ground where peace and jus - tice meet. Here the love of God, through Je - sus, is re - vealed in time and space; as we share in Christ the feast that frees us:

4 Let us build a house where hands will reach be - yond the wood and stone to heal and strength - en, serve and teach, and live the Word they've known. Here the out - cast and the strang - er bear the im - age of God's face; let us bring an end to fear and dan - ger:

5 Let us build a house where all are named, their songs and vi - sions heard and loved and trea - sured, taught and claimed as words with - in the Word. Built of tears and cries and laugh - ter, prayers of faith and songs of grace, let this house pro - claim from floor to raf - ter:

All are wel - come, **all** are wel - come,

all are wel - come in this place.

Text: Marty Haugen, b. 1950

Music: Two Oaks 9 6 8 6 8 7 10 and refrain, Marty Haugen

Text and music © 1994 GIA Publications, Inc. All rights reserved.

R 220

Will You Let Me Be Your Servant

1 Will you let me be your ser - vant,
2 We are pil - grims on a jour - ney,
3 I will hold the Christ - light for you

4 I will weep when you are weep - ing;
5 When we sing to God in heav - en
6 Will you let me be your ser - vant,

let me be as Christ to you? Pray that I may
we are trav - 'lers on the road; we are here to
in the night - time of your fear; I will hold my

when you laugh I'll laugh with you. I will share your
we shall find such har - mo - ny, born of all we've
let me be as Christ to you? Pray that I may

have the grace to let you be my ser - vant, too.
help each oth - er walk the mile and bear the load.
hand out to you, speak the peace you long to hear.

joy and sor - row till we've seen this jour - ney through.
known to - geth - er of Christ's love and ag - o - ny.
have the grace to let you be my ser - vant, too.

Text: Richard Gillard, b. 1953
Music: THE SERVANT SONG   8 7 8 7, Richard Gillard
Text and music © 1977 Scripture In Song, admin. Integrity Music/ASCAP

Rise, O Sun of Righteousness

1 Rise, O Sun of righ - teous - ness! With your
2 Rouse our hearts from slum - ber deep; may your
3 Gath - er in your scat - tered flock; give us
4 Burst the bars of stub - born pride; make the
5 Hon - or, praise, and glo - ry be to the

might cre - a - tion bless. Shine up - on your church to - day,
word with - in us leap. Give us voic - es to pro - claim
wat - er from the rock. Bless the u - ni - ty we share
heav'n - ly path - way wide. Raise us up from sin and death
Ho - ly Trin - i - ty! May your gra - cious will be done:

show - ing all your gen - tle way. Have mer - cy, Lord.
prais - es to your ho - ly name. Have mer - cy, Lord.
in our shep - herd's lov - ing care. Have mer - cy, Lord.
with your Spir - it's liv - ing breath. Have mer - cy, Lord.
make us one, as you are one. Have mer - cy, Lord.

Text: Christian David, 1691–1751, et al.; tr. Frank W. Stoldt, b. 1958

Music: SONNE DER GERECHTIGKEIT 7 7 7 7 4, Bohemian Brethren, *Kirchengeseng*, 1566

Text © 2003 Augsburg Fortress

R 222

This Is a Day, Lord, Gladly Awaited

1 This is a day, Lord, glad-ly a-wait - ed; thank-ful our
2 Bless now their vows, Lord, seal-ing com-mit - ment; deep-en their
3 Sow in their hearts, Lord, seeds of com-pas - sion; reap in their
4 Hal-low the years, Lord, they spend to-geth - er, grow-ing in

hearts, Lord, joy-ous our praise. See here be - fore you two whom we
trust, Lord, lov-ing-ly won. Work-ing your won-ders, knit them to-
lives, Lord, care for your earth. May they en-cour-age oth-ers by
love, Lord, as you in - tend; free - ly for-giv-ing, time with-out

cher - ish; keep them be - side you all of their days.
geth - er so noth-ing sun - ders two be-come one.
be - ing signs of God's new age com-ing to birth.
num - ber; self - less - ly liv - ing, time with-out end.

Text: Jeffery Rowthorn, b. 1934
Music: BUNESSAN 5 5 8 D, Gaelic traditional; arr. B. Wayne Bisbee, b. 1934
Text © Jeffery Rowthorn
Arr. © 1995 Augsburg Fortress

In Christ Called to Baptize

R 223

1 In Christ called to bap - tize, we wit - ness to grace,
2 In Christ called to ban - quet, one ta - ble we share,
3 In Christ called to wit - ness, by grace we will preach
4 U - nite us, a - noint us, O Spir - it of love,

and gath - er a peo - ple from each land and race.
a ha - ven of wel - come, a cir - cle of care.
the life - giv - ing gos - pel; God's love we will teach.
for you are with - in us, a - round us, a - bove.

In deep, flow - ing wa - ters, we share in Christ's death,
Al - though we are man - y, we share in one bread.
By grace may our liv - ing give proof to our praise
E - quip us for ser - vice with gifts you be - stow.

then, ris - ing to new life, give thanks with each breath.
One cup of thanks - giv - ing pro - claims Christ, our head.
in cost - ly com - pas - sion re - flect - ing Christ's ways.
In Christ is our call - ing. In Christ may we grow.

Text: Ruth Duck, b. 1947
Music: St. Denio   11 11 11 11, Welsh traditional
Text © 1995 Ruth Duck, admin. GIA Publications, Inc. All rights reserved.

R 224

Build Us Up, Lord

1 Build us up, Lord, build us up; set in
2 Build us up, Lord, build us up; let our

us a strong foun - da - tion. Lead us to do your
lives re - flect your glo - ry. Cast a - way all our

ho - ly will; form and shape your new cre - a - tion.
doubts and fears; help us tell the world your sto - ry.

Build us up, Lord, build us up; as we
Build us up, Lord, build us up; as we

guide and teach each oth - er, help us to share your love with the
bear good fruit for you, Lord, give us vi - sion and keep us

world: ev - 'ry sis - ter, ev - 'ry broth - er.
sure. Grant us faith that's stead - fast and true.

Refrain

Grow - ing in Christ, we plant seeds for the king - dom; we fol - low in

faith what's be - gun! Lord, set in our hearts the

pow'r of your word to spread the news of your Son!

Grow-ing in Christ, we plant seeds for the king-dom; we fol-low in

faith what's be - gun! Lord, set in our hearts the

pow'r of your word to spread the news of your Son!

Text: Mark Glaeser and Donna Hanna
Music: BUILD US UP, Mark Glaeser and Donna Hanna
Text and music © 2003 Augsburg Fortress

Heaven Is Singing for Joy
El cielo canta alegría

1 Heav-en is sing-ing for joy, al-le-lu - ia,
2 Heav-en is sing-ing for joy, al-le-lu - ia,
3 Heav-en is sing-ing for joy, al-le-lu - ia,

1 El cie-lo can-ta_a-le-grí - a, ¡a-le-lu - ya!,
2 El cie-lo can-ta_a-le-grí - a, ¡a-le-lu - ya!,
3 El cie-lo can-ta_a-le-grí - a, ¡a-le-lu - ya!,

for in your life and in mine is shin-ing the glo-ry of God.
for in your heart and in mine a-bides the one love of our God.
for in your world and in mine we tell the good news of our God.

por-que_en tu vi - da_y la mí - a bri - lla la glo-ria de Dios.
por-que_a tu vi - da_y la mí - a las u-ne_el a-mor de Dios.
por - que tu vi - da_y la mí - a pro - cla-mar - án al Se - ñor.

Refrain / Estribillo

Al - le - lu - ia, al - le-lu - ia! Al - le -
¡A - le - lu - ya, a - le-lu - ya! ¡A - le -

lu - ia, al - le-lu - ia!
lu - ya, a - le-lu - ya!

Text: Pablo Sosa, b. 1933
Music: ALEGRÍA, Pablo Sosa
Text and music © Pablo Sosa

There Is a Name I Love to Hear

R 226

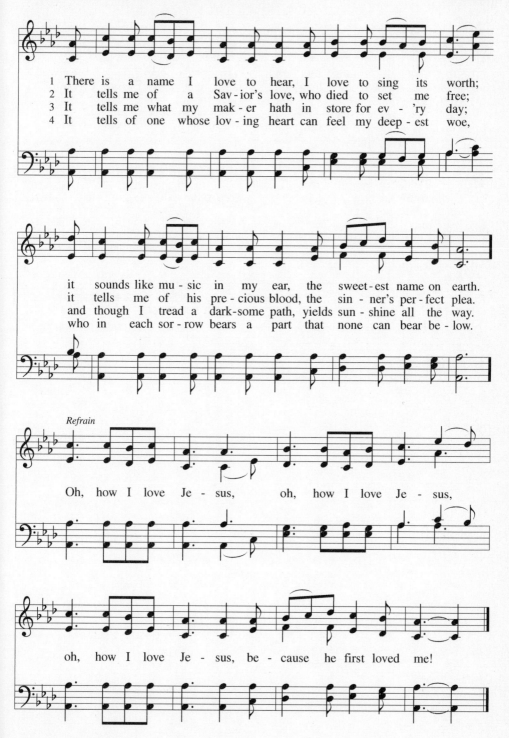

1 There is a name I love to hear, I love to sing its worth;
2 It tells me of a Sav-ior's love, who died to set me free;
3 It tells me what my mak-er hath in store for ev-'ry day;
4 It tells of one whose lov-ing heart can feel my deep-est woe,

it sounds like mu-sic in my ear, the sweet-est name on earth.
it tells me of his pre-cious blood, the sin-ner's per-fect plea.
and though I tread a dark-some path, yields sun-shine all the way.
who in each sor-row bears a part that none can bear be-low.

Refrain

Oh, how I love Je - sus, oh, how I love Je - sus,

oh, how I love Je - sus, be - cause he first loved me!

Text: Frederick Whitfield, 1829–1904
Music: OH, HOW I LOVE JESUS C M and refrain, North American traditional, 19th cent.

R 227   This Is the Threefold Truth

1 This is the three-fold truth on which our faith de-pends;
2 Made sa-cred by long use, new-mint-ed for our time,
3 On this we fix our minds as, pray-ing side by side,
4 By this we are up-held when doubt or grief as-sails
5 This is the three-fold truth which, if we hold it fast,

and with this joy-ful cry wor-ship be-gins and ends:
our li-tur-gies sum up the hope we have in him:
we take the bread and wine from Christ, the Cru-ci-fied:
our Chris-tian for-ti-tude, and on-ly grace a-vails:
chang-es the world and us and brings us home at last.

Refrain

Christ has died! Christ is ris-en! Christ will come a-gain!

Text: Fred Pratt Green, 1903–2000

Music: THREEFOLD TRUTH   6 6 6 6 and refrain, William P. Rowan, b. 1951

Bring Forth the Kingdom

R 228

Leader

1 You are salt for the earth, O peo-ple: salt for the king-dom of God!
2 You are a light on the hill, O peo-ple: light for the cit-y of God!
3 You are a seed of the word, O peo-ple: bring forth the king-dom of God!
4 We are a blest and a pil-grim peo-ple: bound for the king-dom of God!

Leader ... **All**

Share the fla-vor of life, O peo-ple: life in the king-dom of God!
Shine so ho-ly and bright, O peo-ple: shine for the king-dom of God!
Seeds of mer-cy and seeds of jus-tice, grow in the king-dom of God!
Love our jour-ney and love our home-land: love is the king-dom of God!

Refrain

Bring forth the king-dom of mer-cy, bring forth the

king-dom of peace; bring forth the king-dom of jus-tice,

bring forth the cit-y of God!

Text: Marty Haugen, b. 1950
Music: BRING FORTH THE KINGDOM   9 7 9 7 and refrain, Marty Haugen
Text and music © 1986 GIA Publications, Inc. All rights reserved.

R 229

We Raise Our Hands to You

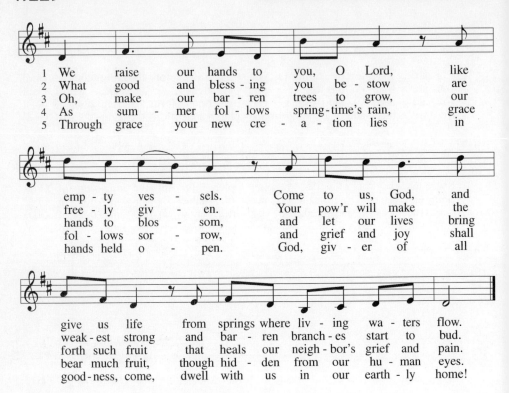

1 We raise our hands to you, O Lord, like
2 What good and bless - ing you be - stow are
3 Oh, make our bar - ren trees to grow, our
4 As sum - mer fol - lows spring-time's rain, grace
5 Through grace your new cre - a - tion lies in

emp - ty ves - sels. Come to us, God, and
free - ly giv - en. Your pow'r will make the
hands to blos - som, and let our lives bring
fol - lows sor - row, and grief and joy shall
hands held o - pen. God, giv - er of all

give us life from springs where liv - ing wa - ters flow.
weak - est strong and bar - ren branch - es start to bud.
forth such fruit that heals our neigh - bor's grief and pain.
bear much fruit, though hid - den from our hu - man eyes.
good - ness, come, dwell with us in our earth - ly home!

Text: Svein Ellingsen, b. 1929; tr. Hedwig T. Durnbaugh, b. 1929
Music: VI REKKER VÅRE HENDER FREM 8 5 8 8, Trond Kverno, b. 1945
Music © 1978 Norsk Musikforlag A/S
English text © Hedwig T. Durnbaugh

To God Our Thanks We Give

Reamo leboga

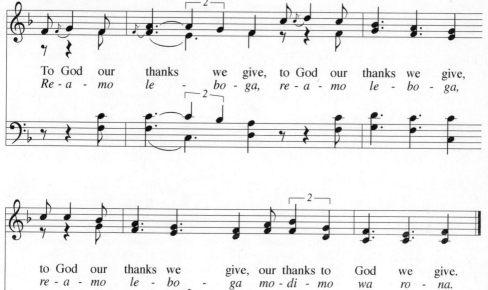

To God our thanks we give, to God our thanks we give,
Re - a - mo le - bo - ga, re - a - mo le - bo - ga,

to God our thanks we give, our thanks to God we give.
re - a - mo le - bo - ga mo - di - mo wa ro - na.

Text: Botswanan traditional, taught by Daisy Nshakazongwe Tswana; tr. I-to Loh, b. 1936
Music: REAMO LEBOGA   6 6 6 6, Botswanan traditional; taught by Daisy Nshakazongwe Tswana
Text and music © 1986 World Council of Churches and the Asian Institute for Liturgy and Music

R 231

Count Your Blessings

1 When up - on life's bil - lows you are tem - pest - toss'd,
2 Are you ev - er bur - den'd with a load of care?
3 When you look at oth - ers with their lands and gold,
4 So, a - mid the con - flict, wheth - er great or small,

when you are dis - cour - aged, think - ing all is lost,
Does the cross seem heav - y you are called to bear?
think that Christ has prom - ised you his wealth un - told;
do not be dis - heart - en'd, God is o - ver all;

count your man - y bless - ings, name them one by one,
Count your man - y bless - ings, ev - 'ry doubt will fly,
count your man - y bless - ings, wealth can nev - er buy
count your man - y bless - ings, an - gels will at - tend,

and it will sur - prise you what the Lord has done.
and you will keep sing - ing as the days go by.
your re - ward in heav - en, nor your home on high.
help and com - fort give you to your jour - ney's end.

Count your blessings, name them one by one;
Count your man-y bless-ings,
name them one by one;

count your blessings, see what God has done!
count your man-y bless-ings,
see what God has done!

Count your bless-ings, name them one by one;
Count your man-y bless-ings,

and it will sur-prise you what the Lord has done.

Text: Johnson Oatman Jr., 1856–1922
Music: BLESSINGS 11 11 11 11 and refrain, Edwin O. Excell, 1851–1921

R 232

We Are an Offering

We lift our voic-es, we lift our hands, we lift our lives up to you: we are an of-fer-ing. Lord, use our voic-es, Lord, use our

hands, Lord, use our lives, they are yours: we are an of-fer-ing. All that we have, all that we are, all that we hope to be, we

give to you, we give to you. We lift our voic-es, we lift our hands, we lift our lives up to you: we are an of-fer-ing, we are an of-fer-ing.

Text: Dwight Liles, b. 1957
Music: OFFERING, Dwight Liles

As Saints of Old

R 233

1 As saints of old their first - fruits brought of or - chard, flock, and
2 A world in need now sum - mons us to la - bor, love, and
3 In grat - i - tude and hum - ble trust we bring our best to -

field to God, the giv - er of all good, the source of boun - teous
give; to make our life an of - fer - ing to God, that all may
day to serve your cause and share your love with all a - long life's

yield; so we to - day first - fruits would bring, the
live. The church of Christ is call - ing us to
way. O God, who gave your - self to us in

wealth of this good land, of farm and mar - ket,
make the dream come true: a world re - deemed by
Je - sus Christ your Son, teach us to give our -

shop and home, of mind and heart and hand.
Christ - like love; all life in Christ made new.
selves each day un - til life's work is done.

Text: Frank von Christierson, 1900–1996
Music: FOREST GREEN C M D, English traditional
Text © 1961, ren. 1989 The Hymn Society, admin. Hope Publishing Co. All rights reserved.

R 234

By the Waters of Babylon

high - est joy. 3 For the wick - ed car - ried us a - way, cap -
tiv - i - ty re - quired from us a song.
How can we sing our ho - ly song in a strange
land? For the wick - ed car - ried us a - way, cap - tiv - i - ty re -
quired from us a song. How can we sing our
ho - ly song in a strange land? So let the words of my
mouth and the med - i - ta - tions of my heart be ac -
cept-a - ble in your sight, O God.

Text: Jamaican traditional, sts. 1 and 3; Marian Dolan, st. 2
Music: Jamaican Psalm 137 Jamaican traditional
Text st. 2 © 2002 Augsburg Fortress

R 235

In Deepest Night

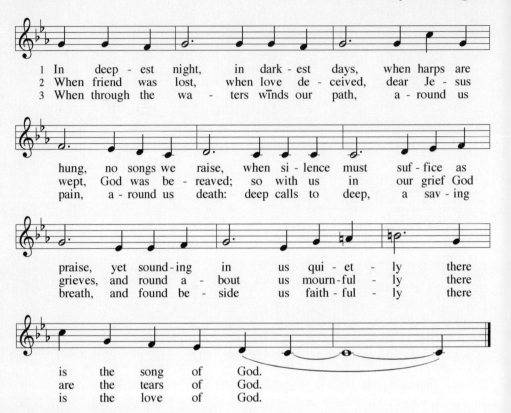

1 In deep-est night, in dark-est days, when harps are
2 When friend was lost, when love de-ceived, dear Je-sus
3 When through the wa-ters winds our path, a-round us

hung, no songs we raise, when si-lence must suf-fice as
wept, God was be-reaved; so with us in our grief God
pain, a-round us death: deep calls to deep, a sav-ing

praise, yet sound-ing in us qui-et-ly there
grieves, and round a-bout us mourn-ful-ly there
breath, and found be-side us faith-ful-ly there

is the song of God.
are the tears of God.
is the love of God.

Text: Susan Palo Cherwien, b. 1953

Music: DEEP BLUE   8 8 8 8 6, Thomas Pavlechko, b. 1962

Text © 1995 Susan Palo Cherwien, admin. Augsburg Fortress

Music © 2002 Selah Publishing Co. All rights reserved.

In Suffering Love the Thread of Life

1 In suf - f'ring love the thread of life is
2 There is a rock, a place se - cure with -
3 In love's deep womb our fears are held; there
4 Lord, to our hearts your joy com - mit, in -
5 In suf - f'ring love our God comes now, hope's

wo - ven through our care, for God is with us;
in the storm's cold blast; con - cealed with - in the
God's rich tears are sown and bring to birth, in
to our hands your pain; so send us out to
vi - sion born in gloom; with tears and laugh - ter

not a - lone our pain and toil we bear.
suf - f'ring night God's cov - e - nant stands fast.
hope new - born, the strength to jour - ney on.
touch the world with bless - ings in your name.
shared and blessed the des - ert yet will bloom.

Text: Rob W. Johns, 1941–1986
Music: HIDING PLACE   C M, J. Leavitt, *Christian Lyre*, 1830
Text © 1987 Elinor Johns, admin. Augsburg Fortress

R 237

When Pain of the World Surrounds Us

1 When pain of the world sur - rounds us with dark - ness and de -
2 We see with fear and trem - bling our ach - ing world in
3 The church is a ho - ly ves - sel the liv - ing wa - ters
4 We praise you for our jour - ney and your a - bun - dant

spair, when search - ing just con - founds us with
need, con - fess - ing to each oth - er our
fill to nour - ish all its peo - ple, God's
grace, your sav - ing word that guid - ed a

false hopes ev - 'ry - where, when lives are starved for mean - ing and
waste-ful - ness and greed. May we with stead - fast car - ing the
pur - pose to ful - fill. May we with hum - ble cour - age be
strug - gling hu - man race. O God, with all cre - a - tion, your

des - ti - ny is bare, we are called to fol - low Je - sus and
hun - gry chil - dren feed. We are called to fol - low Je - sus and
o - pen to God's will. We are called to fol - low Je - sus and
fu - ture we em - brace. We are called to fol - low Je - sus and

let God's heal - ing flow through us.
let God's jus - tice flow through us.
let God's Spir - it flow through us.
let God's chang - es flow through us.

Text: Jim Strathdee, b. 1941
Music: CALLED TO FOLLOW, Jim Strathdee
Text and music © 1978 Desert Flower Music

How Long, O God

1 "How long, O God?" the psalm - ist cries, a
2 The e - vil lurks with - in, with - out, it
3 Your grace, O God, seems far a - way; will
4 How can we hope? How can we sing? O
5 "How long, O God?" the psalm - ist cries, a

cry we make our own, for we are lost, a -
threat - ens to de - stroy the frag - ile cords that
heal - ing ev - er come? Our bro - ken lives lie
God, set free our voice to name the sor - rows,
cry we make our own. Though we are lost, a -

lone, a - fraid, and far a - way from home.
make us one, that bind our hearts in joy.
bro - ken still; will night give way to dawn?
name the pain, that we might yet re - joice.
lone, a - fraid, our God will lead us home.

Text: Ralph F. Smith, 1950–1994
Music: LAND OF REST   C M, North American traditional
Text © 2003 Augsburg Fortress

R 239

Goodness Is Stronger than Evil

Good-ness is stron-ger than e - vil; love is stron-ger than hate;

light is stron-ger than dark - ness; life is stron-ger than death; vic-t'ry is

Oh,

ours, vic-t'ry is ours, through him who loved us.

vic-t'ry is ours, vic-t'ry is ours, through him who loved us.

Text: from *An African Prayer Book*, selected by Desmond Tutu, b. 1931

Music: GOODNESS IS STRONGER 8 6 7 6 4 4 5, John L. Bell, b. 1949

Come to Be Our Hope, O Jesus
Vem, Jesus nossa esperança

1 Come to be our hope, O Je - sus; come to
2 Come to build your new cre - a - tion through the

1 Vem, Je - sus nos - sa_es - pe - ran - ça, nos - sas
2 Vem te - cer um mun - do_no - vo nos cam - in -

set your peo - ple free. From op - pres - sion come, re -
road of ser - vant - hood; give new life to ev - 'ry

vi - das li - ber - tar. Vem, nas - cer em nós, cri -
hos da ver - da - de; para que, a - fin - al, o

lease us; all your pow - er let us see. Come, re -
na - tion, chang - ing e - vil in - to good. Come and

an - ça, vem o teu po - der nos dar. Vem, li -
po - vo vi - va_em plen li - ber - da - de. Vem, Je -

lease from ev - 'ry pris - on those who
o - pen our to - mor - row for a

ber - ta_os prio - sio - nei - ros da_in - jus -
sus, abre o fu - tu - ro do teu

suf - fer in our land. In your love we find the
king - dom, now so near. Take a - way all hu - man

ti - ça_e da_a - fli - çó; vem, re - ú - ne_os bra - si
re - ino de_al - ger - ia. Vem, der - ru - ba_o_i - men - so

rea - son still to live and un - der - stand.
sor - row, give us hope a - gainst our fear.

lei - ros em a - mor e_em - com - preen - só.
mu - ro que sep - a - ra_a noite e_o dia.

Text: Jaci Maraschin
Music: JESUS NOSSA ESPERANÇA 8 7 8 7 D, Marcílio de Oliveira Filho
Portuguese text and music © 1978 Jaci Maraschin, Sao Paulo, Brazil
English text © 1989 World Council of Churches

R 241

A Place at the Table

1. For ev - 'ry - one born, a place at the ta - ble, for
2. For wom - an and man, a place at the ta - ble, re -
3. For young and for old, a place at the ta - ble, a
4. For just and un - just, a place at the ta - ble, a -
5. For ev - 'ry - one born, a place at the ta - ble, to

ev - 'ry - one born, clean wa - ter and bread, a
vis - ing the roles, de - cid - ing the share, with
voice to be heard, a part in the song, the
bus - er, a - bused, with need to for - give, in
live with - out fear, and sim - ply to be, to

shel - ter, a space, a safe place for grow - ing, for
wis - dom and grace, di - vid - ing the pow - er, for
hands of a child in hands that are wrin - kled, for
an - ger, in hurt, a mind - set of mer - cy, for
work, to speak out, to wit - ness and wor - ship, for

ev - 'ry - one born, a star o - ver - head.
wom - an and man, a sys - tem that's fair.
young and for old, the right to be - long.
just and un - just, a new way to live.
ev - 'ry - one born, the right to be free.

Refrain

And God will de - light when we are cre - a - tors of jus - tice and joy, yes, God will de - light when we are cre - a - tors of jus - tice, jus - tice and joy!

Text: Shirley Erena Murray, b. 1931
Music: A PLACE AT THE TABLE   11 10 11 10 and refrain, Lori True

R 242

Let Justice Roll like a River

Refrain

Let jus - tice roll like a riv - er, and wash all op -

pres - sion a - way. Come, O God, and take us,

move and shake us; come now, and make us a - new,

that we might live just - ly like you.

1 "Take from me your ho - ly feasts, all your

of - f'rings and your mu - sic. Let jus - tice

flow like wa - ters, and in - teg - ri - ty like an

Refrain

ev - er - flow - ing stream."

Stanzas 2-5

2 How long shall we wait, O God, for the day of your

3 Hear this, all of you who use the poor in your thirst of
4 "E - ven now, re - turn to me, let your hearts be

5 You have been told the way of life, the way of

mer - cy to dawn, the day we beat our

pow - er and rich - es: the Lord will turn your
bro - ken and hum - ble, for I am gra - cious,

jus - tice and peace: to act just - ly, to

Refrain

swords in - to plows, when your peace reigns o - ver the earth?

laugh - ter to tears, on the won - drous Day of our God.
gen - 'rous and kind." Come and seek the mer - cies of God.

love gent - ly, to walk hum - bly with God.

Text: Marty Haugen, b. 1950
Music: Let Justice Roll, Marty Haugen

Forgive Us, Lord
Perdón, Señor

1 Wind and cold roar through the cit-y street; some folk have no
1 Co - rre_el vien-to_en es - ta gran ciu-dad, mu - chos tem - bla -

heat: for - give us, Lord. Man-y have warm homes, wool clothes to
rán: per - dón, Se - ñor. Pa - ra u - nos hoy ha - brá ca -

wear; this is so un - fair: for - give us, Lord.
lor, pa - ra o - tros, no: per - dón, Se - ñor.

Refrain/Estribillo

Help us grasp how this is our sin; teach us,
A - yú - da - nos a en - ten - der nues - tra

save us by your cross, for the things we crave and seek to
cul - pa, oh Se - ñor. Nues-tras a - le - grí - as son do -

win cost our neigh-bors loss. For - give us, Lord.
lor pa - ra mu-chos hoy: per - dón, Se - ñor.

2 Those within may swell with civic pride;
many wait outside: forgive us, Lord.
Some have many chances to succeed;
others live in need: forgive us, Lord.

3 Violence and hatred, near and far,
terror, slaughter, war: forgive us, Lord.
You insist the hungry shall be fed;
let us give them bread: forgive us, Lord.

2 *Esta gran ciudad progresará,*
muchos sufrirán: perdón, Señor.
Para unos, la_oportunidad,
para otros, no: perdón, Señor.

3 *Guerras y más guerras por la paz,*
muchos morirán: perdón, Señor.
Muchas manos se levantarán
reclamando pan; perdón, Señor.

Text: Homero Perera; tr. Madeleine Forell Marshall, b. 1946
Music: CORRE EL VIENTO 9 5 4 9 5 4 and refrain, Homero Perera
Spanish text and music © 1968 Homero R. Perera
English text © 2003 Madeleine Forell Marshall, admin. Augsburg Fortress

For the Life of the World

Text: David Haas, b. 1957

Music: David Haas; arr. Jeanne Cotter, b. 1964

R 245

Canticle of the Turning

1 My soul cries out with a joy - ful shout that the
2 Though I am small, my God, my all, you
3 From the halls of power to the for - tress tower, not a
4 Though the na - tions rage from age to age, we re -

God of my heart is great, and my spir - it sings of the
work great things in me, and your mer - cy will last from the
stone will be left on stone. Let the king be - ware for your
mem - ber who holds us fast: God's mer - cy must de -

won - drous things that you bring to the ones who wait. You
depths of the past to the end of the age to be. Your
jus - tice tears ev - 'ry ty - rant from his throne. The
liv - er us from the con - quer - or's crush - ing grasp. This

fixed your sight on your ser - vant's plight, and my
ver - y name puts the proud to shame, and to
hun - gry poor shall weep no more, for the
sav - ing word that our fore - bears heard is the

weak - ness you did not spurn, so from east to west shall my
those who would for you yearn, you will show your might, put the
food they can nev - er earn; there are ta - bles spread, ev - 'ry
prom - ise which holds us bound, till the spear and rod can be

name be blest. Could the world be a - bout to turn?
strong to flight, for the world is a - bout to turn.
mouth be fed, for the world is a - bout to turn.
crushed by God, who is turn - ing the world a - round.

Refrain

My heart shall sing of the day you bring. Let the

fires of your jus - tice burn. Wipe a - way all tears, for the

dawn draws near, and the world is a - bout to turn.

Text: Rory Cooney, b. 1952, based on the Magnificat
Music: STAR OF COUNTY DOWN, Irish traditional

R 246

When Our Song Says Peace

1 When our song says peace and the world says war, we will
2 When our song says free and the world says bound, we will
3 When our song says home and the world says lost, we will

sing de-spite the world. We will trust the song, for we sing of God, who
sing de-spite the world. We will trust the song, for we sing of God, who
sing de-spite the world. We will trust the song, for we sing of God, who

breaks the spear and sword and stills the storm of war.
o - pens pris - on doors and sets the cap - tives free.
brings us home at last, and gives a song to all.

Text: Richard Leach, b. 1953

Music: JENKINS   10 7 10 6 6, Thomas Pavlechko, b. 1962

O Christ, Your Heart, Compassionate

R 247

1 O Christ, your heart, com-pas-sion-ate, bore ev-'ry hu-man pain.
2 As once you wel-comed those cast down and healed the sick, the blind,
3 O Christ, cre-ate new hearts in us that beat in time with yours,
4 O Love that made the dis-tant stars, yet mark the spar-row's fall,

Its beat-ing was the pulse of God; its breadth, God's vast do-main.
so may all bruised and bro-ken lives through us your help still find.
that joined by faith with your great heart be-come love's o-pen doors.
whose arms stretched wide up-on a cross em-brace and bear us all:

The heart of God, the heart of Christ, com-bined in per-fect rhyme,
Lord, join our hearts with those who weep that none may weep a-lone,
We are your bod-y, ris-en Christ; our hearts, our hands we yield
come, make your church a ser-vant church that walks your ser-vant ways,

to write God's love in hu-man deeds, e-ter-ni-ty in time.
and help us bear an-oth-er's pain as though it were our own.
that through our life and min-is-try your love may be re-vealed.
whose deeds of love rise up to you, a sac-ri-fice of praise!

Text: Herman G. Stuempfle Jr., b. 1923
Music: ELLACOMBE 7 6 7 6 D, M.V. Werkmeister, *Gesangbuch der Herzogl. Hofkapelle*, 1784
Text © 2000 GIA Publications, Inc. All rights reserved.

R 248

Let Streams of Living Justice

1 Let streams of liv-ing jus-tice flow down up-on the earth;
2 Your ci-ty's built to mu-sic; we are the stones you seek;

give free-dom's light to cap-tives, let all the poor have worth.
your har-mo-ny is lan-guage; we are the words you speak.

The hun-gry's hands are plead-ing, the work-ers claim their rights,
Our faith we find in ser-vice, our hope in oth-er's dreams,

the mourn-ers long for laugh-ter, the blind-ed seek for sight.
our love in hand of neigh-bor; our home-land bright-ly gleams.

Make lib-er-ty a bea-con, strike down the i-ron pow'r;
In-scribe our hearts with jus-tice; your way—the path un-tried;

a-bol-ish an-cient ven-geance: pro-claim your peo-ple's hour.
your truth—the heart of strang-er; your life—the Cru-ci-fied.

Text: William Whitla, b. 1934
Music: THAXTED 13 13 13 13 13 13, Gustav Theodore Holst, 1874–1934
Text © 1989 William Whitla

R 249

When the Poor Ones
Cuando el pobre

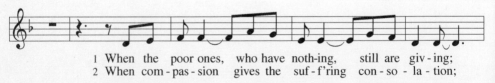

1 When the poor ones, who have noth-ing, still are giv-ing;
2 When com-pas-sion gives the suf-f'ring con-so-la-tion;

1 Cuan-do_el po-bre na-da tie-ne y_aún re-par-te,
2 Cuan-do_al-gu-no su-fre_y lo-gra su con-sue-lo,

when the thirst - y   pass the   cup,   wa - ter to   share;
when ex - pect - ing   brings to   birth   hope that was   lost;
cuan - do   al - guien pa - sa   sed   y_a - gua nos   da,
cuan - do_es - pe - ra_y   no se   can - sa de_es - pe - rar,

when the wound - ed   of - fer   oth - ers   strength and heal - ing:
when we choose love,   not the   ha - tred   all   a - round us:
cuan - do_el dé - bil   a su_her-ma - no   for - ta - le - ce,
cuan - do_a - ma - mos,   aun-que_el o - dio   nos   ro - de - e,

Refrain / Estribillo

we see   God,   here   by   our   side,   walk - ing our
va Dios   mis - mo_en   nues - tro   mis - mo   ca - mi -

way;   we   see   God,   here   by   our
nar;   va Dios   mis - mo_en   nues - tro

side,   walk - ing   our   way.
mis - mo   ca - mi - nar.

3 When our spirits, like a chalice, brim with gladness;
   when our voices, full and clear, sing out the truth;
   when our longings, free from envy, seek the humble:

4 When the goodness poured from heaven fills our dwellings;
   when the nations work to change war into peace;
   when the stranger is accepted as our neighbor:

3 Cuando crece la_alegría_y nos inunda,
   cuando dicen nuestros labios la verdad,
   cuando_amamos el sentir de los sencillos,

4 Cuando_abunda_el bien y llena los hogares,
   cuando_alguien donde_hay guerra pone paz,
   cuando_"hermano" le llamamos al extraño,

Spanish text: J.A. Olivar, b. 1939; English text: Martin A. Seltz, b. 1951

Music: EL CAMINO   12 11 12 11 11, Miguel Manzano and J. A. Olivar

Text and music © 1971, 1998 J.A. Olivar, Miguel Manzano and San Pablo Internacional—SSP, admin. OCP Publications.

R 250

Light Dawns on a Weary World

1 Light dawns on a wea-ry world when eyes be-gin to see all
2 Love grows in a wea-ry world when hun-gry hearts find bread and
3 Hope blooms in a wea-ry world when crea-tures, once for-lorn, find

peo-ple's dig-ni-ty. Light dawns on a
chil-dren's dreams are fed. Love grows in a
wil-der-ness re-born. Hope blooms in a

wea-ry world: the prom-ised day of jus-tice comes.
wea-ry world: the prom-ised feast of plen-ty comes.
wea-ry world: the prom-ised green of E-den comes.

Refrain

The trees shall clap their hands; the dry lands, gush with springs; the hills and

moun-tains shall break forth with sing-ing! We shall go

out in joy, and be led forth in peace, as all the

world in won-der ech-oes sha-lom.

Text: Mary Louise Bringle, b. 1953
Music: TEMPLE OF PEACE 7 6 7 7 8, William P. Rowan, b. 1951
Text © 2002 GIA Publications, Inc. All rights reserved.
Music © 2000 William P. Rowan, admin. GIA Publications, Inc.

We Are Called

R 251

1 Come!   Live   in   the   light!
2 Come!   O - pen   your   heart!
3 Sing!   Sing   a   new   song!

Shine   with the   joy   and   the   love   of   the   Lord!   We   are
Show   your . . .   mer - cy   to   all   those   in   fear!   We   are
Sing   of   that   great day   when   all   will   be   one!   God   will

called   to   be   light   for   the   king - dom,   to
called   to   be   hope   for   the   hope - less   so   all
reign,   and   we'll   walk   with   each   oth - er   as

live   in   the   free - dom   of   the   cit - y   of   God.
ha - tred and   blind - ness   will   be . . .   no   more.
sis - ters and   broth - ers   u - nit - ed   in   love.

Refrain

We   are   called   to   act   with   jus - tice,   we   are   called   to

love   ten - der - ly;   we   are   called   to   serve   one   an -

oth-er,   to   walk   hum - bly   with   God.

Text: David Haas, b. 1957
Music: We Are Called, David Haas

R 252

God, Whose Farm Is All Creation

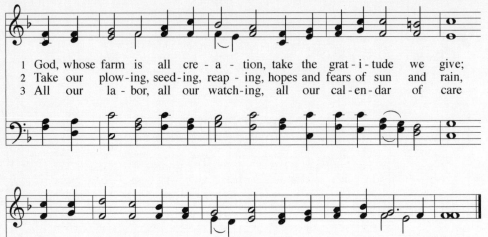

1 God, whose farm is all cre - a - tion, take the grat - i - tude we give;
2 Take our plow - ing, seed - ing, reap - ing, hopes and fears of sun and rain,
3 All our la - bor, all our watch - ing, all our cal - en - dar of care

take the fin - est of our har - vest, crops we grow that we may live.
all our think - ing, plan - ning, wait - ing, rip - ened in this fruit and grain.
in these crops of your cre - a - tion, take, O God: they are our prayer.

Text: John Arlott, 1914–1991
Music: OMNI DIE 8 7 8 7, *Gross Catolisch Gesangbuch*, Nürnberg, 1631
Text © Trustees of the late John Arlott

When at Last the Rain Falls
Al caer la lluvia

R 253

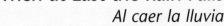

1 When at last the rain falls, our world turns liv - ing green.
2 All the pret - ty song - birds re - joice and sing your praise,

1 Al ca - er la llu - via re - sur - ge con ver - dor
2 El co - quí se_a - le - gra, se sien - te, muy fe - liz;

Lit - tle flow - ers blos - som, the air is warm and clean.
war - ble hymns ex - qui - site, through sun - ny spring-time days.

to - da la flo - res - ta. ¡Re - nue - va la crea - ción!
can - ta_en su_a - la - ban - za: "co - quí, co - quí, co - quí."

See the gor-geous lil - y its ra - diant blooms dis - play;
Night - in - gales and tree-frogs sing praise when it grows dark,
Mi - ra_el ro - jo li - rio; el duen - de ya bro - tó.
El pi - ti - rre can - ta y tri - na_el rui - se - ñor.

may I just as bold - ly praise God in my own way.
on - ly cease at day - break, and then we hear the lark.
¡Be - lla pri - ma - ve - ra que_a-nun - cia su ful - gor!
¡Cuán a - le - gre - men - te a - la - ban al Crea - dor!

Refrain/Estribillo

All the lit - tle flow - ers and ten - der curl - ing ferns
To - da flor sil - ves - tre, la ma - ya el cun - dea - mor:

show their mak-er's glo - ry, each praise to God re - turns.
¡Có - mo ma - ni - fies - tan la glo - ria del Se - ñor!

Sing, all of cre - a - tion, your mak - er prais - es ac - cord!
¡Có - mo se te_a - la - ba en tod - a la cre - a - ción!

I al - so will of - fer my songs to you, O Lord.
Yo qui - sie - ra_ha-cer - lo en for - ma_i - gual, Se - ñor.

Spanish text: Pablo Fernández-Badillo, b. 1919; English text: Madeleine Forell Marshall, b. 1946
Music: ALABANZA   12 12 D and refrain, Pablo Fernández-Badillo
Spanish text and music © Pablo Fernández Badillo
English text © 2003 Madeleine Forell Marshall, admin. Augsburg Fortress

R 254

Touch the Earth Lightly

1 Touch the earth light - ly, use the earth gent - ly,
3 Let there be green - ing, birth from the burn - ing,
4 God of all liv - ing, God of all lov - ing,

nour-ish the life of the world in our care:
wa - ter that bless - es and air that is sweet,
God of the seed - ling, the snow and the sun,

gift of great won - der, ours to sur - rend - er,
health in God's gar - den, hope in God's chil - dren,
teach us, de - flect us, Christ re - con - nect us,

trust for the chil - dren to - mor - row will bear. *To st. 2*
re - gen - er - a - tion that peace will com - plete.
us - ing us gent - ly, and mak - ing us one.

2 We who en - dan - ger, who cre - ate hun - ger,

a - gents of death for all crea-tures that live,

we who would fos - ter clouds of dis - as - ter—

D.C. for sts. 3 and 4

God of our plan - et, fore - stall and for - give!

Text: Shirley Erena Murray, b. 1931
Music: TENDERNESS 5 5 10 D, Colin Gibson, b. 1933

God, the Sculptor of the Mountains

R 255

1 God the sculp-tor of the moun-tains, God the mill-er of the
2 God the nui-sance to the Pha-raoh, God the cleav-er of the
3 God the dress-er of the vine-yard, God the plant-er of the
4 God the un-ex-pect-ed in-fant, God the calm, de-ter-mined

sand, God the jewel-er of the heav - ens,
sea, God the pil-lar in the dark - ness,
wheat, God the reap-er of the har - vest,
youth, God the ta-ble-turn-ing proph - et,

God the pot-ter of the land: you are womb of all cre-
God the bea-con of the free: you are fount of all de-
God the source of all we eat: you are host at ev-'ry
God the re-sur-rect-ed truth: you are pres-ent ev-'ry

a - tion, we are form-less; shape us now.
liv - 'rance, we are sight-less; lead us now.
ta - ble, we are hun-gry; feed us now.
mo - ment, we are search-ing; meet us now.

Text: John Thornburg, b. 1954

Music: JENNINGS-HOUSTON 8 7 8 7 8 7, Amanda Husberg, b. 1940

Text © 1993 John Thornburg

R 256

God Created Heaven and Earth

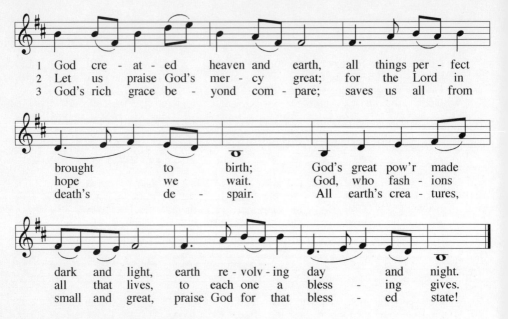

1 God cre - at - ed heaven and earth, all things per - fect
2 Let us praise God's mer - cy great; for the Lord in
3 God's rich grace be - yond com - pare; saves us all from

brought to birth; God's great pow'r made
hope we wait. God, who fash - ions
death's de - spair. All earth's crea - tures,

dark and light, earth re - volv - ing day and night.
all that lives, to each one a bless - ing gives.
small and great, praise God for that bless - ed state!

Text: Taiwanese traditional; tr. Boris Anderson, b. 1918, and Clare Anderson, b. 1923

Music: TŌA-SĪA, Piⁿ-po' melody, Taiwanese traditional

Tr. © Boris and Clare Anderson, admin. Christian Conference of Asia

Your Will Be Done

Mayenziwe

Text: South African, from the Lord's Prayer

Music: MAYENZIWE 8 8 8 8 8 8, South African traditional; taught by Gobingca Mxadana; transc. John L. Bell, b. 1949

R 258

Lord, Listen to Your Children

On bend-ed knee, with need-y hearts, we come and pray. Lord, lis-ten to your chil-dren.

With will-ing hearts and o-pen arms, we come and pray. Lord, lis-ten to your chil-dren. With sim-ple words of heart-felt thanks, we come. Be-liev-ing in your prom-is-es, we come. On bend-ed knee, with need-y hearts, we come and pray. Lord, lis-ten to your chil-dren, lis-ten to your chil-dren.

Text: Handt Hanson, b. 1950
Music: On Bended Knee, Handt Hanson; arr. Henry Wiens, b. 1951
Text and music © 1991 Prince of Peace Publishing, Changing Church, Inc.

It's Me, O Lord

Refrain

It's me, it's me, O Lord, stand-in' in the need of prayer;
it's me,

it's me, it's me, O Lord, stand-in' in the need of prayer.
it's me,

1 Not my broth - er, not my sis - ter, but it's me, O Lord,
2 Not the preach - er, not the dea - con, but it's me, O Lord,
3 Not my fa - ther, not my moth - er, but it's me, O Lord,
4 Not the strang - er, not my neigh - bor, but it's me, O Lord,

stand-in' in the need of prayer; not my broth - er, not my sis - ter, but it's
stand-in' in the need of prayer; not the preach-er, not the dea - con, but it's
stand-in' in the need of prayer; not my fa - ther, not my moth - er, but it's
stand-in' in the need of prayer; not the strang - er, not my neigh-bor, but it's

Refrain

me, O Lord, stand - in' in the need of prayer.
me, O Lord, stand - in' in the need of prayer.
me, O Lord, stand - in' in the need of prayer.
me, O Lord, stand - in' in the need of prayer.

Text: African American spiritual
Music: STANDING IN THE NEED   13 7 13 7 and refrain, African American spiritual

R 260

O God in Heaven

1 O God in heav-en, grant to your chil-dren mer-cy and
2 Je-sus, re-deem-er, help us re-mem-ber your pain and
3 Spir-it un-end-ing, give us your bless-ing: strength for the

bless-ing, songs nev-er ceas-ing, grace to in-vite us, peace to u-
pas-sion, your res-ur-rec-tion, your call to fol-low, your love to-
wea-ry, help for the need-y, hope for the scorn-ful, peace for the

nite us— O God in heav-en, au-thor of love.
mor-row— Je-sus, re-deem-er, sav-ior, and friend.
mourn-ful— Spir-it un-end-ing, com-fort and guide.

Text: Elena G. Maquiso; tr. D.T. Niles, alt.

Music: HALAD 5 5 5 5, Philippines traditional, adapt. Elena G. Maquiso; arr. *Cantate Domino*, 1980

Lord, Be Glorified

R 261

1 In my life, Lord, be glo-ri-fied, be glo-ri-fied;
2 In my song, Lord, be glo-ri-fied, be glo-ri-fied;
3 In your church, Lord, be glo-ri-fied, be glo-ri-fied;

in my life, Lord, be glo-ri-fied to-day.
in my song, Lord, be glo-ri-fied to-day.
in your church, Lord, be glo-ri-fied to-day.

Text: Bob Kilpatrick, b. 1952

Music: BE GLORIFIED   4 4 4 4 4 6, Bob Kilpatrick

R 262

Just a Closer Walk with Thee

Refrain

Just a clos-er walk with thee, grant it, Je-sus, is my plea;

dai-ly walk-ing close to thee, let it be, dear Lord, let it be.

1. I am weak but thou art strong: Je-sus, keep me from all wrong;
2. Through this world of toil and snares, if I fal-ter, Lord, who cares?
3. When my fee-ble life is o'er, time for me will be no more;

Refrain

I'll be sat-is-fied as long as I walk, let me walk close to thee.
Who with me my bur-den shares? None but thee, dear . . Lord, none but thee.
guide me gent-ly, safe-ly o'er to thy king-dom . . shore, to thy shore.

Text: North American traditional
Music: CLOSER WALK, North American traditional

Calm to the Waves

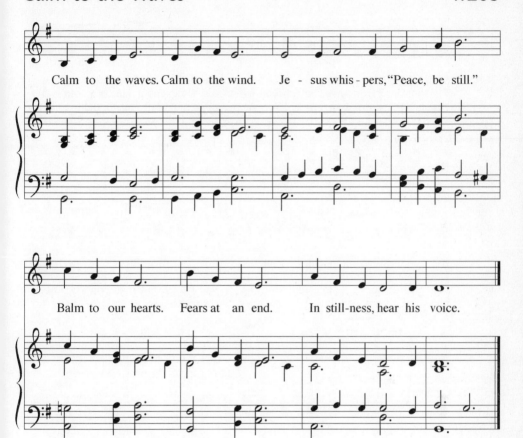

Calm to the waves. Calm to the wind. Je - sus whis - pers, "Peace, be still."

Balm to our hearts. Fears at an end. In still-ness, hear his voice.

Text: Mary Louise Bringle, b. 1953
Music: CALM SEAS 4 4 7 4 4 7, Thomas Pavlechko, b. 1962

R 264

Savior, like a Shepherd Lead Us

1 Sav-ior like a shep-herd lead us; much we need your ten-der care.
2 We are yours; in love be-friend us, be the guard-ian of our way;
3 You have prom-ised to re-ceive us, poor and sin-ful though we be;
4 Ear-ly let us seek your fa - vor, ear-ly let us do your will;

In your pleas-ant pas-tures feed us, for our use your fold pre-pare.
keep your flock, from sin de-fend us, seek us when we go a-stray.
you have mer-cy to re-lieve us, grace to cleanse, and pow'r to free.
bless-ed Lord and on-ly Sav-ior, with your love our spir-its fill.

Bless-ed Je-sus, bless-ed Je-sus, you have bought us; we are yours.
Bless-ed Je-sus, bless-ed Je-sus, hear us chil-dren when we pray.
Bless-ed Je-sus, bless-ed Je-sus, ear-ly let us turn to you.
Bless-ed Je-sus, bless-ed Je-sus, you have loved us, love us still.

Bless-ed Je-sus, bless-ed Je-sus, you have bought us; we are yours.
Bless-ed Je-sus, bless-ed Je-sus, hear us chil-dren when we pray.
Bless-ed Je-sus, bless-ed Je-sus, ear-ly let us turn to you.
Bless-ed Je-sus, bless-ed Je-sus, you have loved us, love us still.

Text: Dorothy A. Thrupp, 1779–1847
Music: BRADBURY 8 7 8 7 D, William B. Bradbury, 1816–1868

Holy, Holy, Holy
Santo, santo, santo

Ho-ly, ho-ly, ho-ly, ho-ly, ho-ly, ho-ly is our God,
San-to, san-to, san-to, san-to, san-to es nues-tro Dios,

God, the Lord of earth and heav-en. Ho-ly, ho-ly is our God.
Se-ñor de to-da la tie-rra. San-to, san-to es nues-tro Dios.

Ho-ly, ho-ly, ho-ly, ho-ly, ho-ly, ho-ly is our God,
San-to, san-to, san-to, san-to, san-to es nues-tro Dios,

Fine

God, the Lord of all of his-t'ry. Ho-ly, ho-ly is our God.
Se-ñor de to-da la his-to-ria. San-to, san-to es nues-tro Dios.

Who ac-com-pa-nies our peo-ple, who lives with-in our strug-gles,
Que a-com-pa-ña a nues-tro pue-blo, que vi-ve en nues-tras lu-chas,

of all the earth and heav-en the one and on-ly Lord.
del u-ni-ver-so en-te-ro el ú-ni-co Se-ñor.

Bless-ed those who in the Lord's name an-nounce the ho-ly gos-pel,
Ben-di-tos los que en su nom-bre el e-van-ge-lio a-nun-cian,

D.C. al fine

pro-claim-ing the good news that our lib-er-a-tion comes.
la bue-na y gran no-ti-cia de la li-be-ra-ción.

Text: Guillermo Cuéllar, b. 1955; tr. Linda McCrae
Music: CUÉLLAR, Guillermo Cuéllar, b. 1955
Text and tune © 1996 GIA Publications, Inc. All rights reserved.

R 266

Lead Me, Guide Me

Refrain

Lead me, guide me, a - long the way;

for if you lead me, I can - not stray.

Lord, let me walk each day with thee.

Lead me, O Lord, lead me.

1 I am weak and I need thy strength and pow'r
2 Help me tread in the paths of righ - teous - ness,
3 I am lost if you take your hand from me,

to help me o - ver my weak - est hour.
be my aid when Sa - tan and sin op - press.
I am blind with - out ... thy light to see.

Help me through the dark - ness thy face to see.
I am put - ting all .... my trust in thee.
Lord, just al - ways let me thy ser - vant be.

Refrain

Lead me, O Lord, lead me.

Text: Doris Akers, 1922–1995
Music: LEAD ME, GUIDE ME, Doris Akers; arr. Richard Smallwood, b. 1948

R 267

Come to Me, All Pilgrims Thirsty

1 "Come to me, all pil - grims thirst - y; drink the wa - ter I will give.
2 "Come to me, all trav - 'lers wea - ry; come that I may give you rest.
3 "Come to me, be - liev - ers bur - dened; find re - fresh-ment in this place.
4 "Come to me, re - pen - tant sin - ners; leave be - hind your guilt and shame.
5 "Come to me, dis-tressed and need - y; I would be your trust - ed friend.
6 "Come to me, a - ban-doned, or - phaned; lone - ly ways no long - er roam.

If you knew what gift I of - fer, you would come to me and live."
Drink the cup of life I of - fer; at this ta - ble be my guest."
If you knew the gift I of - fer, you would turn and seek my face."
If you knew di - vine com-pas - sion, you would turn and call my name."
If you seek the gift I of - fer, come, your o - pen hands ex - tend."
If you knew the gift I of - fer, you would make in me your home."

Refrain

Je - sus, ev - er - flow-ing foun - tain, give us wa - ter from your well.

In the gra - cious gift you of - fer there is joy no tongue can tell.

Text: Delores Dufner OSB, b. 1939
Music: BEACH SPRING 8 7 8 7 D, *The Sacred Harp*, Philadelphia, 1844; arr. Ronald A. Nelson, b. 1927
Text © 1992, 1996 Sisters of St. Benedict
Arr. © 1978 *Lutheran Book of Worship*, admin. Augsburg Fortress

My Shepherd, You Supply My Need

R 268

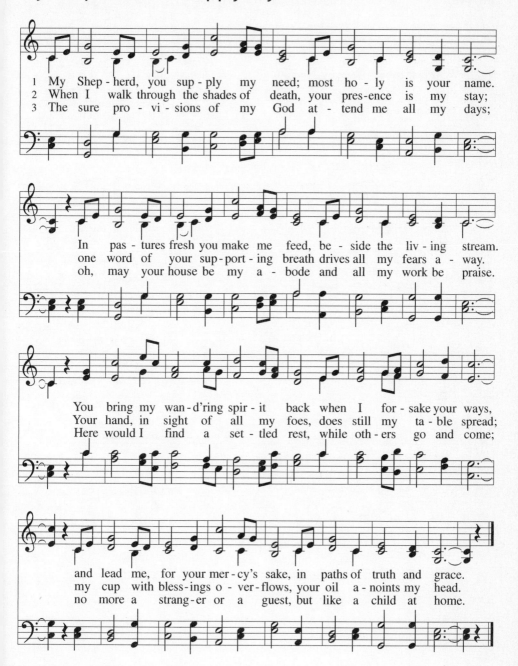

1 My Shep-herd, you sup-ply my need; most ho-ly is your name.
2 When I walk through the shades of death, your pres-ence is my stay;
3 The sure pro-vi-sions of my God at-tend me all my days;

In pas-tures fresh you make me feed, be-side the liv-ing stream.
one word of your sup-port-ing breath drives all my fears a-way.
oh, may your house be my a-bode and all my work be praise.

You bring my wan-d'ring spir-it back when I for-sake your ways,
Your hand, in sight of all my foes, does still my ta-ble spread;
Here would I find a set-tled rest, while oth-ers go and come;

and lead me, for your mer-cy's sake, in paths of truth and grace.
my cup with bless-ings o-ver-flows, your oil a-noints my head.
no more a strang-er or a guest, but like a child at home.

Text: Isaac Watts, 1674–1748, alt.
Music: RESIGNATION L M D, North American traditional

R 269

We've Come This Far by Faith

Refrain

We've come this far by faith, lean-ing on the Lord; trust-ing in his ho - ly word, he's nev - er failed us yet. Oh, can't turn a - round, we've come this far by faith. We've come this far by faith.

1 Just   re - mem - ber   the   good things   God   has
2 Don't   be   dis - cour - aged   with   trou - ble   in   your

done,   things   that   seemed im - pos - si - ble;   oh,
life;   he'll   bear   your   bur - dens,   and

Refrain

praise him for   the vic - t'ries he   has   won.   Oh!   We've
move   all   the dis - cord   and   strife.

Text: Albert A. Goodson
Music: This Far by Faith, Albert A. Goodson
Text and music © 1965, renewed 1993 by Manna Music, Inc. All rights reserved.

R 270

When Memory Fades

1 When mem-'ry fades, and rec-og-ni-tion fal-ters, when eyes we love grow dim, and minds con-fused, speak to our souls of love that nev-er al-ters; speak to our hearts, by pain and fear a-bused. O God of life and heal-ing peace, em-pow'r us with pa-tient cour-age, by your grace in-fused.

2 As frail-ness grows, and youth-ful strengths di-min-ish, in wea-ry arms which worked their ear-nest fill, your ag-ing ser-vants la-bor now to fin-ish their earth-ly tasks, as fits your mer-cy's will. We grieve their wan-ing, yet re-joice, be-liev-ing, your arms, un-wea-ried, shall up-hold us still.

3 With-in your Spir-it, good-ness lives un-fad-ing. The past and fu-ture min-gle in-to one. All joys re-main, un-shad-owed light per-vad-ing. No val-ued deed will ev-er be un-done. Your mind en-folds all fi-nite acts and off-'rings. Held in your heart, our death-less life is won.

Text: Mary Louise Bringle, b. 1953
Music: FINLANDIA 11 10 11 10 11 10, Jean Sibelius, 1865–1957; arr. Gunnar J. Malmin, *Concordia Hymnal*, 1932
Text © 2002 by GIA Publications, Inc. All rights reserved. Arr. © 1932 Augsburg Publishing House

As the Deer

As the deer pants   for   the wa-ter, so my soul longs af - ter you;

you a - lone are my heart's de - sire   and I   long to wor - ship you.

Refrain

You a-lone are my strength and shield; to you a-lone may my spir-it   yield.

You a - lone are my heart's de - sire   and I   long   to wor - ship you.

Text: Martin J. Nystrom, b. 1956

Music: AS THE DEER   8 7 8 7 8 9 8 7, Martin J. Nystrom

Text and music © 1984 Maranatha Praise, Inc., admin. The Copyright Company. All rights reserved. International copyright secured.

R 272

Shepherd Me, O God

Refrain

Shep-herd me, O God, be-yond my wants, be-yond my fears, from

to stanzas 1, 2, 3, 5

death in - to life.

to stanza 4

life.

1 God is my shep-herd, so noth-ing shall I want, I
2 Gent - ly you raise me and heal my wea - ry soul, you
3 Though I should wan - der the val - ley of death, I

rest in the mead-ows of faith - ful - ness and love, I
lead me by path-ways of righ-teous-ness and truth, my
fear no e - vil, for you are at my side, your

Refrain

walk by the qui - et wa - ters of peace.
spir - it shall sing the mu - sic of your name.
rod and your staff, my com - fort and my hope.

4 You have set me a ban-quet of love in the face of ha - tred,

Refrain

crown-ing me with love be - yond my pow'r to hold.

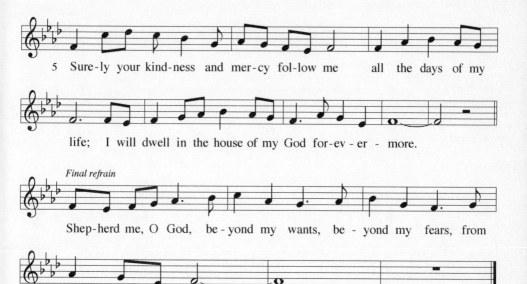

5 Sure-ly your kind-ness and mer-cy fol-low me all the days of my

life; I will dwell in the house of my God for-ev - er - more.

Final refrain

Shep-herd me, O God, be - yond my wants, be - yond my fears, from

death in - to life.

Text: Marty Haugen, b. 1950
Music: SHEPHERD ME, Marty Haugen
Text and music © 1986 GIA Publications, Inc. All rights reserved.

R 273

What God Ordains Is Good Indeed

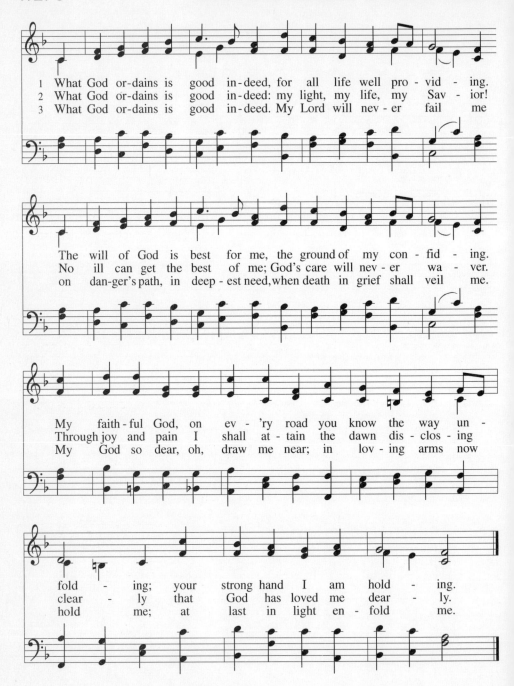

1 What God or-dains is good in-deed, for all life well pro-vid - ing.
2 What God or-dains is good in-deed: my light, my life, my Sav - ior!
3 What God or-dains is good in-deed. My Lord will nev-er fail me

The will of God is best for me, the ground of my con - fid - ing.
No ill can get the best of me; God's care will nev-er wa - ver.
on dan-ger's path, in deep - est need, when death in grief shall veil me.

My faith-ful God, on ev - 'ry road you know the way un -
Through joy and pain I shall at - tain the dawn dis - clos - ing
My God so dear, oh, draw me near; in lov - ing arms now

fold - ing; your strong hand I am hold - ing.
clear - ly that God has loved me dear - ly.
hold me; at last in light en - fold me.

Text: Samuel Rodigast, 1649–1708; tr. Martin A. Seltz, b. 1951
Music: WAS GOTT TUT   8 7 8 7 8 8 8, Severus Gastorius, 1646–1682
Text © 2000 Augsburg Fortress

Glory, Glory, Hallelujah!

1 Glo - ry, glo - ry, hal - le - lu - jah!
2 I feel bet - ter, so much bet - ter,
3 Feel like shout - ing, "Hal - le - lu - jah!"
4 I am climb - ing Ja - cob's lad - der,
5 Ev - 'ry round goes higher and high - er,

since I laid my bur - den down.
since I laid my bur - den down.
since I laid my bur - den down.
since I laid my bur - den down.
since I laid my bur - den down.

Glo - ry, glo - ry, hal - le - lu - jah!
I feel bet - ter, so much bet - ter,
Feel like shout - ing, "Hal - le - lu - jah!"
I am climb - ing Ja - cob's lad - der,
Ev - 'ry round goes higher and high - er,

since I laid my bur - den down.
since I laid my bur - den down.
since I laid my bur - den down.
since I laid my bur - den down.
since I laid my bur - den down.

Text: African American spiritual
Music: GLORY GLORY HALLELUJAH   8 7 8 7, African American spiritual; arr. Carl Haywood, b. 1949
Arr. from *The Haywood Collection of Negro Spirituals* © 1992 Carl Haywood

R 275

Change My Heart, O God

Change my heart, O God; make it ev - er true.

Change my heart, O God; may I be like you.

You are the pot - ter; I am the clay.

Mold me and make me; this is what I pray.

Change my heart, O God; make it ev - er true.

Change my heart, O God; may I be like you.

Text: Eddie Espinosa, b. 1953
Music: CHANGE MY HEART, Eddie Espinosa
Text and music © 1982 Mercy/Vineyard Publishing (ASCAP)

Will You Come and Follow Me
The Summons

1 "Will you come and fol - low me if I but call
2 "Will you leave your - self be - hind if I but call
3 "Will you let the blind - ed see if I but call
4 "Will you love the you you hide if I but call
5 Lord, your sum - mons ech - oes true when you but call

your name? Will you go where you don't
your name? Will you care for cruel and
your name? Will you set the pris - 'ners
your name? Will you quell the fear in -
my name. Let me turn and fol - low

know and nev - er be the same?
kind and nev - er be the same?
free and nev - er be the same?
side and nev - er be the same?
you and nev - er be the same.

Will you let my love be shown, will you let my
Will you risk the hos - tile stare, should your life at -
Will you kiss the lep - er clean, and do such as
Will you use the faith you've found to re - shape the
In your com - pa - ny I'll go where your love and

name be known, will you let my life be
tract or scare? Will you let me an - swer
this un - seen, and ad - mit to what I
world a - round, through my sight and touch and
foot - steps show. Thus I'll move and live and

grown in you and you in me?"
pray'r in you and you in me?"
mean in you and you in me?"
sound in you and you in me?"
grow in you and you in me.

Text: John L. Bell, b. 1949

Music: KELVINGROVE 13 13 7 7 13, Scottish traditional

R 277 — Lord Jesus, You Shall Be My Song

1 Lord Je - sus, you shall be my song as I jour - ney;
2 Lord Je - sus, I'll praise you as long as I jour - ney.
1 Jé - sus, je vou - drais te chan - ter sur ma rou - te;
2 Jé - sus, je vou - drais te lou - er sur ma rou - te;

I'll tell ev - 'ry - bod - y a - bout you wher - ev - er I go:
May all of my joy be a faith - ful re - flec - tion of you.
Jé - sus, je vou - drais t'an - non - cer à mes voi - sins par - tout,
Jé - sus, je vou - drais que ma voix soit l'é - cho de ta joie,

you a - lone are our life and our peace and our love.
May the earth and the sea and the sky join my song.
car toi seul es la vie et la paix et l'a - mour:
et que chan - te la terre et que chan - te le ciel;

Lord Je - sus, you shall be my song as I jour - ney.
Lord Je - sus, I'll praise you as long as I jour - ney.
Jé - sus, je vou - drais te chan - ter sur ma rou - te.
Jé - sus, je vou - drais te lou - er sur ma rou - te.

Text: Les Petites Soeurs de Jésus and L'Arche Community; tr. Stephen Somerville, b. 1931
Music: LES PETITES SOEURS 12 14 12 12, Les Petites Soeurs de Jésus and L'Arche Community
Text © Les Petites Soeurs de Jésus; tr. © 1970 Stephen Somerville
Music © 1987 Les Petites Soeurs de Jésus

3   As long as I live, Jesus, make me your servant,
     to carry your cross and to share all your burdens and tears.
     For you saved me by giving your body and blood.
     As long as I live, Jesus, make me your servant.

4   I fear in the dark and the doubt of my journey;
     but courage will come with the sound of your steps by my side.
     And with all of the family you saved by your love,
     we'll sing to your dawn at the end of our journey.

3   *Jésus, je voudrais te servir sur ma route,*
     Jésus, je voudrais partager les soufrances de ta croix,
     car tu livres pour moi et ton corps et ton sang;
     Jésus, je voudrais te servir su ma route.

4   *Jésus, je voudrais tour au long de ma route,*
     entendre tes pas résonner dans le nuit près de moi,
     jusqu'à l'aube du jour où ton peuple sauvé,
     Jésus, chantera ton retour sur ma route.

Take, Oh, Take Me As I Am   R 278

Text and music: John L. Bell, b. 1949

Make Me a Channel of Your Peace
Hazme un instrumento de tu paz

1 Make me a chan-nel of your peace.
2 Make me a chan-nel of your peace.
4 Make me a chan-nel of your peace.

1 *Haz - me_un ins - tru - men - to de tu paz:*
2 *Haz - me_un ins - tru - men - to de tu paz;*
4 *Haz - me_un ins - tru - men - to de tu paz;*

Where there is ha - tred, let me bring your
Where there's de - spair in life, let me bring
It is in par - don - ing that we are

don - de_ha - ya o - dio lle - ve yo tu_a -
que lle - ve tu_es - pe - ran - za por do -
es per - do - nan - do que nos das per -

love; where there is in - ju -
hope; where there is dark - ness,
par - doned, in giv - ing of our -

mor, don - de_ha - ya_in - ju - ria,
quier; don - de_ha - ya_os - cu - ri -
dón, es dan - do_a to - dos

last time to Coda ⊕

ry, your par - don, Lord; and
.... on - ly light; and
selves that we re -

tu per - dón, Se - ñor, don -
dad, lle - ve tu luz, don -
que ... tu nos

|1

where there's doubt, true faith in you.
where there's sad - ness, ev - er joy.

de_ha - ya du - da, fe, Se - ñor, en ti.
de_ha - ya pe - na, tu go - zo, Se - ñor.

2

3 O Mas - ter, grant that I may nev - er
3 *Ma - es - tro, a - yú - da - me a nun - ca bus -*

seek   so much to be con - soled as to con -
car   quer - er ser con - so - la - do, si - no

sole,   to be un - der - stood
con - so - lar;   ser en - ten - di - do

as to un - der - stand,   to be
si - no en - ten - der,   ser a -

D.C. (stanza 4) al coda

loved as to love with all my soul.
ma - do   si - no yo a - mar.

Coda

ceive   and in dy - ing that we're
das;   y mu - rien - do es que vol -

born to e - ter - nal life.
ve - mos a na - cer.

Text: Sebastian Temple, b. 1928
Music: PRAYER OF ST. FRANCIS, Sebastian Temple
Text and music © 1967 OCP Publications. All rights reserved.

Blessed Be the Name
Heri ni jina

1 Bless-ed be the name, bless-ed be the name, bless-ed be the name, Je-sus' name.
2 Let us go to Je-sus, let us go to Je-sus, let us go to Je-sus in heav'n.

1 He - ri ni ji - na, he - ri ni ji - na, he - ri ni ji - na la Ye - su.
2 Twen-de kwa Ye - su, twen-de kwa Ye - su, twen-de kwa Ye - su mbin-gu - ni.

Bless-ed be the name, bless-ed be the name, bless-ed be the name, Je-sus' name. Be-lieve!
Let us go to Je-sus, let us go to Je-sus, let us go to Je-sus in heav'n.

He - ri ni ji - na, he - ri ni ji - na, he - ri ni ji - na la Ye - su. A-mi-ni!
Twen-de kwa Ye - su, twen-de kwa Ye - su, twen-de kwa Ye - su mbin-gu - ni.

Al - le - lu - ia, al - le - lu - ia. Bless-ed be the name, Je-sus' name. Be-lieve!
Al - le - lu - ia, al - le - lu - ia. Let us go to Je-sus in heav'n.

Al - le - lu - ya, al - le - lu - ya. He - ri ni ji - na la Ye - su. A - mi - ni!
Al - le - lu - ya, al - le - lu - ya. Twen-de kwa Ye - su mbin-gu - ni.

Al - le - lu - ia, al - le - lu - ia. Bless-ed be the name, Je-sus' name.
Al - le - lu - ia, al - le - lu - ia. Let us go to Je-sus in heav'n.

Al - le - lu - ya, al - le - lu - ya. He - ri ni ji - na la Ye - su.
Al - le - lu - ya, al - le - lu - ya. Twen-de kwa Ye - su mbin-gu - ni.

Text: taught by Deogratias Mahamba
Music: HERI NI JINA, east African traditional, arr. Mark Sedio
Text and music © 2003 Augsburg Fortress

Have Thine Own Way, Lord

1 Have thine own way, Lord, have thine own way.
2 Have thine own way, Lord, have thine own way.
3 Have thine own way, Lord, have thine own way.
4 Have thine own way, Lord, have thine own way.

Thou art the pot - ter, I am the clay.
Search me and try me, Mas - ter, to - day.
Wound - ed and wea - ry, help me, I pray.
Hold o'er my be - ing ab - so - lute sway.

Mold me and make me af - ter thy will,
Pur - er than snow, Lord, wash me just now,
Pow - er, all pow - er sure - ly is thine.
Fill with thy Spir - it till all shall see

while I am wait - ing, yield - ed and still.
as in thy pres - ence hum - bly I bow.
Touch me and heal me, Sav - ior di - vine.
Christ on - ly, al - ways, liv - ing in me.

Text: Adelaide A. Pollard, 1862–1934
Music: ADELAIDE 5 4 5 4 D, George C. Stebbins, 1846–1945

Take My Life, That I May Be
Toma, oh Dios, mi voluntad

R 282

Refrain/Estribillo

Take my life, that I may be con - se - crat - ed, Lord, to thee;
To - ma, oh Dios, mi vo - lun - tad, y haz - la tu - ya, na - da más;

take my mo - ments and my days; let them flow in cease-less praise.
to - ma, sí, mi co - ra - zón y tu tro - no en él ten - drás.

1 Take my hands and let them move
2 Take my sil - ver and my gold,

1 Que mi vi - da en te - ra es - té
2 Que mis pies tan só - lo en pos

at the im - pulse of thy love;
not a mite would I with - hold;

con - sa - gra - da a tí, Se - ñor;
de lo san - to pue - dan ir,

Refrain/Estribillo

take my feet and let them be swift and beau - ti - ful for thee.
take my in - tel - lect and use ev' - ry pow'r as thou shall choose.

que a mis ma - nos pue - da guiar el im - pul - so de tu a - mor.
y que a ti, Se - ñor, mi voz, se com - plaz - ca en ben - de - cir.

3 Take my voice and let me sing
always, only for my King;
take my lips and let them be
filled with messages from thee.

3 Que mis labios al hablar
hablen sólo de tu amor;
que mis bienes dedicar
yo los quiera a tí, Señor.

4 Take my will and make it thine,
it shall be no longer mine;
take my heart, it is thine own,
it shall be thy royal throne.

4 Que mi tiempo todo esté
consagrado a tu loor;
que mi mente y su poder
sean usados en tu honor.

English text: Frances Havergal, 1836–1879; Spanish text: Vicente Mendoza, 1875–1955
Music: TOMA MI VOLUNTAD 7 7 7 7 and refrain, William Dexheimer-Pharris; arr. Mark Sedio, b. 1954
Tune © 1998 Augsburg Fortress; arr. © 1999 Augsburg Fortress

Holy Woman, Graceful Giver

1 Ho - ly wom - an, grace - ful giv - er, proph - et, ser - vant,
2 Like the ves - sel, we are bro - ken; like the oint - ment,
3 In these jars is hid - den trea - sure, cost - ly fra - grance,
4 Ho - ly wom - an, cost - ly trea - sure, with the jar of

and be - liev - er, wom - an with the oint - ment jar,
we are to - ken of God's lov - ing un - to death;
Christ - ly plea - sure, like the Christ, first from the dead,
al - a - bas - ter, shows the hid - den gift we are;

rose up near the time ap - point - ed, broke the seal, Christ's
like the wom - an, we are serv - ing; like the scold - ers,
bro - ken for cre - a - tion's whole - ness, poured out for its
there - fore let us as Christ's ser - vants hold our sis - ter

head a - noint - ed for the com - ing fa - tal hour.
ill de - serv - ing such a rich, for - giv - ing faith.
com - ing full - ness, Proph - et, Ser - vant, Hope, and Head.
in re - mem - brance, wom - an with the oint - ment jar.

Text: Susan Palo Cherwien, b. 1953
Music: ALABASTER 8 8 7 8 8 7, David Cherwien, b. 1957
Text © 1994 Susan Palo Cherwien, admin. Augsburg Fortress
Music © 1995 Augsburg Fortress

R 284

Make a Joyful Noise

Refrain

Make a joy - ful noise all the earth!

Wor - ship your God with glad - ness.

Make a joy - ful noise all the earth.

Come to this place with a song!

1 Know that your God has made you.
2 En - ter these gates, thanks giv - ing.
3 A - ges through end - less a - ges,

Know it's to God we be - long. And
En - ter these courts with praise. Sing
sea - sons of end - less years, the

come to this place with joy - ful-ness and praise.
thanks to your God and bless the ho - ly name.
love of our mak - er ev - er shall en - dure.

Refrain

Wor - ship your God with a song!

Text: Linnea Good, b. 1962
Music: PSALM 100, Linnea Good
Text and music © Borealis Music

Voices Raised to You

R 285

1 Voic - es raised to you we of - fer; tune them, God, for
2 All cre - a - tion joins to praise you; earth and sky your
3 Christ, the song of love in - car - nate, touch-ing earth with
4 Spir - it, flam - ing through cre - a - tion, kin - dle faith with -
5 How can an - y praise we of - fer mea - sure all the

songs of praise. Hearts and hands we bring in trib - ute
works dis - play. Art and mu - sic, gifts you lend us,
heav - en's grace, for your liv - ing, suf - f'ring, dy - ing,
in each heart. Lift our voic - es high in cho - rus;
thanks we owe? Take our hearts and hands and voic - es—

for your gifts through all our days. Al - le - lu - ia!
we re - turn to you to - day. Al - le - lu - ia!
for your ris - ing, hear our praise! Al - le - lu - ia!
through our hands your love im - part. Al - le - lu - ia!
gifts of love we can be - stow. Al - le - lu - ia!

Al - le - lu - ia! Tri - une God, to you we sing!
Al - le - lu - ia! God, cre - a - tor, source of life!
Al - le - lu - ia! Christ, re - deem - er, Lord of life!
Al - le - lu - ia! Spir - it, help - er, breath of life!
Al - le - lu - ia! Tri - une God, to you we sing!

Text: Herman G. Stuempfle Jr., b. 1923
Music: SONG OF PRAISE 8 7 8 7 8 7, Carolyn Jennings, b. 1936

R 286

Holy Ground

We are stand-ing on ho-ly ground,

and I know that there are an-gels all a-round.

Let us praise Je-sus now.

We are stand-ing in his pres-ence on ho-ly ground.

Text: Geron Davis, b. 1960
Music: HOLY GROUND, Geron Davis
Text and music © 1983 Meadowgreen Music Co./Songchannel Music Co., admin. EMI Christian Music Publishing

Praise Ye the Lord

Refrain

Praise ye the Lord, hal - le - lu - jah!

Ev - 'ry - bod - y, praise the Lord.

1 Praise God with the sound of the trum - pet;
2 Praise God with ho - ly cym - bals;
3 Praise God in the ho - ly tem - ple;
4 Praise God on top of the moun - tains;

praise God with the lute and the harp;
praise God with strings and with pipes;
praise God for al - might - y deeds;
praise God both day and night;

praise God with the tim - brel and danc - ing;
praise God with clash - ing cym - bals;
praise God for those boun - ti - ful mer - cies;
praise God down in the low val - leys;

Refrain

praise God wher - ev - er you are.
praise God with all of your might.
for God ful - fills our needs.
praise God be - cause it's all right.

Text: J. Jefferson Cleveland, 1937–1986, alt.

Music: CLEVELAND   8 7 8 7 and refrain, J. Jefferson Cleveland

Text and music © J. Jefferson Cleveland

R 288

I Will Sing, I Will Sing

1 I will sing, I will sing a song un - to the Lord.
2 We will come, we will come as one be - fore the Lord.
3 If the Son, if the Son shall make . . . you . . . free,

4 They that sow in tears . . . . shall reap . . . . in . . . joy.
5 Ev - 'ry knee shall bow . . . and ev - 'ry tongue con - fess,
6 In his name, in his name we have the vic - to - ry.

I will sing, I will sing a song un - to the Lord.
We will come, we will come as one be - fore the Lord.
if the Son, if the Son shall make . . . . you . . . free,

They that sow in tears . . . . shall reap . . . . in . . . joy.
ev - 'ry knee shall bow . . . and ev - 'ry tongue con - fess,
In his name, in his name we have the vic - to - ry.

I will sing, I will sing a song un - to the Lord.
We will come, we will come as one be - fore the Lord.
if the Son, if the Son shall make . . . . you . . . free,

They that sow in tears . . . . shall reap . . . . in . . . joy.
ev - 'ry knee shall bow . . . and ev - 'ry tongue con - fess,
In his name, in his name we have the vic - to - ry.

Al - le - lu - ia, glo - ry to the Lord.
Al - le - lu - ia, glo - ry to the Lord.
you . . . shall be free . . . . in - deed.

Al - le - lu - ia, glo - ry to the Lord.
that . . . Je - sus Christ . . . . is . . . Lord.
Al - le - lu - ia, glo - ry to the Lord.

Refrain

Al - le - lu, al - le - lu - ia, glo - ry to the Lord. Al - le -
lu, al - le - lu - ia, glo - ry to the Lord. Al - le - lu, al - le - lu - ia, glo-
- ry to the Lord. Al - le - lu - ia, glo - ry to the Lord.

Text: Max Dyer
Music: ALLELUIA, GLORY TO THE LORD, Max Dyer
Text and music © 1974 Celebration

R 289

Sing Out, Earth and Skies

Leader

1 Come, O God of   all the earth: come to us, O
2 Come, O God of   wind and flame: fill the earth with
3 Come, O God of   flash - ing light: twin - kling star and
4 Come, O God of   snow and rain: show - er down up -
5 Come, O Jus - tice, come, O Peace: come and shape our

Leader

Righ - teous One;   come, and bring our   love to birth:
righ - teous - ness;   teach us all to   sing your name:
burn - ing sun;   God of day and   God of night:
on the earth;   come, O God of   joy and pain:
hearts a - new;   come and make op - pres - sion cease:

All

in the glo - ry   of your Son.
may our lives your   love con - fess.
in your light we   all are one.
God of sor - row,   God of mirth.
bring us all to   life in you.

Refrain

Sing out, earth and skies! Sing of the God who

loves you! Raise your joy - ful cries!

Dance to the life a - round you!

Text: Marty Haugen, b. 1950
Music: SING OUT 7 7 7 7 and refrain, Marty Haugen
Text and music © 1985 GIA Publications, Inc. All rights reserved.

Lord, I Lift Your Name on High

R 290

Lord, I lift your name on high, Lord, I love to sing your

prais - es. I'm so glad you're in my life,

I'm so glad you came to save us. You came from heav - en to earth

to show the way, from the earth to the cross,

my debt to pay; from the cross to the grave,

from the grave to the sky; Lord, I lift your name on high.

Text: Rick Founds, b. 1954

Music: LORD, I LIFT YOUR NAME, Rick Founds

Text and music © 1989 Maranatha Praise, Inc., admin. The Copyright Company. All rights reserved. International copyright secured.

R 291

Glory and Praise to Our God

Refrain

Glo - ry and praise to our God, who a - lone gives

light to our days. Man - y are the

4th time to stanza 4

bless - ings he bears to those who trust in his ways.

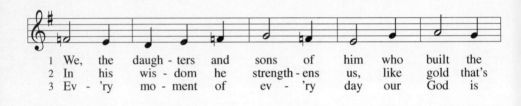

1 We, the daugh - ters and sons of him who built the
2 In his wis - dom he strength - ens us, like gold that's
3 Ev - 'ry mo - ment of ev - 'ry day our God is

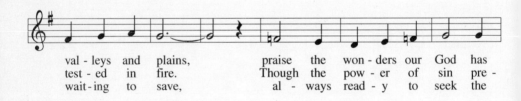

val - leys and plains, praise the won - ders our God has
test - ed in fire. Though the pow - er of sin pre -
wait - ing to save, al - ways read - y to seek the

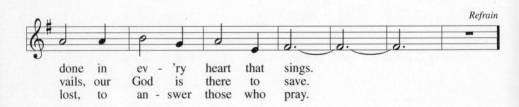

Refrain

done in ev - 'ry heart that sings.
vails, our God is there to save.
lost, to an - swer those who pray.

4 God has wa - tered our bar - ren land and spent his mer - ci - ful rain. Now the riv - ers of life run full for an - y - one to drink.

Final refrain

Glo - ry and praise to our God, who a - lone gives light to our days. Man - y are the bless - ings he bears to those who trust in his ways.

Text: Daniel Schutte, b. 1947
Music: GLORY AND PRAISE, Daniel Schutte

We Have Seen the Lord
Nimemwano Bwana

R 292

Leader

We have seen the Lord.
Ni - me-mwa - no Bwa - na.

God is might-y,
God is low - ly,
God is gra - cious,
Ni - me-mwa - no.

Congregation

We have seen the Lord.
Ni - me - mwa - no Bwa - na.

God is pow-er - ful.
God is mer - ci - ful.
God is won-der - ful.
Ni - me-mwa-no Bwa - na.

We have seen the Lord.
Ni - me - mwa - no Bwa - na.

We have seen the
Ni - me - mwa - no Bwa-

(Fine)

We have seen the Lord.
Ni - me - mwa - no Bwa-na.

Lord, God with us, Je - sus Christ.
na, a na pen de za.

Text: Tanzanian traditional; tr. Jeff Sartain

Music: NIMEMWANO BWANA, Tanzanian traditional, arr. Mark Sedio, b. 1954

Text and music © 2003 Concordia Publishing House

Holy, Holy

R 293

1 Ho - ly, ho - ly, ho - ly, ho - ly,
2 Gra - cious Fa - ther, gra - cious Fa - ther,
3 Pre - cious Je - sus, pre - cious Je - sus,
4 Ho - ly Spir - it, Ho - ly Spir - it,
5 Hal - le - lu - jah, hal - le - lu - jah,

ho - ly, ho - ly, Lord God Al - might - y!
we're so blest to be your chil - dren, gra - cious Fa - ther;
we're so glad that you've re - deemed us, pre - cious Je - sus;
come and fill our hearts a - new, . . . Ho - ly Spir - it;
hal - le - lu - jah, ... hal - le - lu - jah;

and we lift our hearts be - fore you as a to - ken of our love,
and we lift our heads be - fore you as a to - ken of our love,
and we lift our hands be - fore you as a to - ken of our love,
and we lift our voice be - fore you as a to - ken of our love,
and we lift our hearts be - fore you as a to - ken of our love,

ho - ly, ho - ly, ho - ly, ho - ly.
gra - cious Fa - ther, gra - cious Fa - ther.
pre - cious Je - sus, pre - cious Je - sus.
Ho - ly Spir - it, Ho - ly Spir - it.
hal - le - lu - jah, hal - le - lu - jah.

Text: Jimmy Owens, b. 1930
Music: HOLY, HOLY, Jimmy Owens
Text and music © 1972 Communique Music, admin. EMI Christian Music Publishing

R 294   Praise the One Who Breaks the Darkness

1 Praise the One who breaks the dark-ness with a lib - er - at - ing light;
2 Praise the One who blessed the chil - dren with a strong yet gen - tle word;
3 Praise the one true love in - car - nate: Christ, who suf - fered in our place;

praise the One who frees the pris-'ners, turn-ing blind-ness in - to sight.
praise the One who drove out de - mons with a pierc - ing, two - edged sword.
Je - sus died and rose for man - y that we may know God by grace.

Praise the One who preached the gos - pel, heal-ing ev - 'ry dread dis - ease,
Praise the One who brings cool wa - ter to the des - ert's burn-ing sand;
Let us sing for joy and glad-ness, see - ing what our God has done.

calm - ing storms and feed-ing thou-sands with the ver - y bread of peace.
from this well comes liv - ing wa - ter quench-ing thirst in ev - 'ry land.
Praise the one re - deem-ing glo - ry; praise the One who makes us one.

Text: Rusty Edwards, b. 1955
Music: NETTLETON   8 7 8 7 D, Wyeth's *Repository of Sacred Music*, Part II, 1813
Text © 1987 Hope Publishing Co. All rights reserved.

Sing unto the Lord
Chcem oslavovat'

Sing un-to the Lord, praise the ho-ly name, come and praise God with a
Chcem o-sla-vo-vat' svoj-ho Pá - na, chcem Mu spie-vat' no-vú

clap:

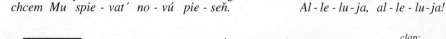

new song. Shout for joy, all the earth,
pie - seň. Chcem ho chva - lit',

clap:

come and praise God with a new song. Al-le-lu-ia, al-le-lu-ia!
chcem Mu spie-vat' no-vú pie-seň. Al-le-lu-ja, al-le-lu-ja!

clap:

Al-le-lu-ia, al-le-lu-ia! Come and praise God with a new song.
Al-le-lu-ja, al-le-lu-ja! Chcem Mu spie-vat' no-vú pie-seň.

Text: Slovak traditional; tr. Mark Sedio, b. 1954
Music: CHCEM OSLAVOVAT', Slovak traditional; arr. Mark Sedio
Tr. and arr. © 2003 Augsburg Fortress

R 296

Shout to the Lord

My Je - sus, my Sav - ior, Lord, there is none like you.

All of my days I want to praise the won-ders of your

might - y love. My com - fort, my shel - ter,

tow-er of ref - uge and strength; let ev-'ry breath, all that I am

nev - er cease to wor - ship you.

Shout to the Lord, all the earth; let us sing pow-er and maj - es-ty, praise

to the King. Moun-tains bow down and the seas will roar at the

sound of your name. I sing for joy at the work

of your hands; for - ev-er I'll love you, for-ev - er I'll stand.

Noth-ing com-pares to the prom - ise I have in you.

Text: Darlene Zschech, b. 1965
Music: SHOUT TO THE LORD, Darlene Zschech
Text and music © 1993 Darlene Zschech/Hillsong Publishing, admin. in the U.S. & Canada by Integrity's Hosanna! Music/ASCAP

R 297

Praise, Praise, Praise the Lord!

Praise, praise, praise the Lord! Praise God's ho - ly name. Al - le - lu - ia!

Praise, praise, praise the Lord! Praise God's ho - ly name. Al - le - lu - ia!

Praise God's ho - ly name. Al - le - lu - ia! Praise God's ho - ly name. Al - le - lu - ia!

Praise God's ho - ly name. Al - le - lu - ia! Praise God's ho - ly name. Al - le - lu - ia!

Text: Cameroon traditional; collected by Elaine Hanson

Music: CAMEROON PRAISE 5 9 5 9 9 9 9 9, Cameroon processional; arr. Ralph M. Johnson

Text and music © 1994 earthsongs

Come, Join the Dance of Trinity

R 298

1 Come, join the dance of Trin-i-ty, be-fore all worlds be-gun—
2 Come, see the face of Trin-i-ty, new-born in Beth-le-hem;
3 Come, speak a-loud of Trin-i-ty, as wind and tongues of flame
4 With-in the dance of Trin-i-ty, be-fore all worlds be-gun,

the in-ter-weav-ing of the Three, the Fa-ther, Spir-it, Son.
then blood-ied by a crown of thorns out-side Je-ru-sa-lem.
set peo-ple free at Pen-te-cost to tell the Sav-ior's name.
we sing the prais-es of the Three, the Fa-ther, Spir-it, Son.

The u-ni-verse of space and time did not a-rise by chance,
The dance of Trin-i-ty is meant for hu-man flesh and bone;
We know the yoke of sin and death, our necks have worn it smooth;
Let voic-es rise and in-ter-weave, by love and hope set free,

but as the Three, in love and hope, made room with-in their dance.
when fear con-fines the dance in death, God rolls a-way the stone.
go tell the world of weight and woe that we are free to move!
to shape in song this joy, this life: the dance of Trin-i-ty.

Text: Richard Leach, b. 1953

Music: KINGSFOLD C M D, English traditional; arr. Ralph Vaughan Williams, 1872–1958

R 299

To God Be the Glory

1 To God be the glo - ry, great things he has done;
2 Oh, per - fect re - demp - tion, the pur - chase of blood,
3 Great things he has taught us, great things he has done,

so loved he the world that he gave us his Son,
to ev - 'ry be - liev - er the prom - ise of God;
and great our re - joic - ing through Je - sus the Son;

who yield - ed his life an a - tone - ment for sin,
the vil - est of - fend - er by grace may be - lieve,
but pur - er, and high - er, and great - er will be

and o - pened the life - gate that all may go in.
that mo - ment from Je - sus a par - don re - ceive.
our won - der, our vic - t'ry, when Je - sus we see.

Refrain

Praise the Lord, praise the Lord, let the earth hear his voice!

Praise the Lord, praise the Lord, let the peo - ple re - joice!

Oh, come to the Fa - ther, through Je - sus the Son,

and give him the glo - ry, great things he has done.

Text: Fanny J. Crosby, 1820–1915
Music: To God Be the Glory 11 11 11 11 and refrain, William H. Doane, 1832–1915

R 300

Soli Deo Gloria

1. O God of bless-ings, all praise to you! Your love sur-
2. All praise for wis-dom, great gift sub-lime, through words and
3. All praise for proph-ets, through grace in-spired to preach and
4. All praise for mu-sic, deep gift pro-found, through hands and

rounds us our whole life through. You are the
teach-ers of ev-'ry time; for stor-ies
wit-ness with hearts on fire. Your Spir-it
voic-es in ho-ly sound; the psalms of

free-dom of those op-pressed; you are the com-fort of all dis-
an-cient and knowl-edge new, for coach-es, men-tors, and coun-s'lors
choos-es the weak and small to sing the new reign where might-y
Da-vid, and Mar-y's praise, in word-less splen-dor and lyr-ic

tressed. Come now, O ho-ly and wel-come guest:
true whose life of ser-vice brought us to you:
fall; with them may we live your gos-pel call:
phrase, with all cre-a-tion one song we raise:

So-li De-o glo-ri-a! So-li De-o glo-ri-a!

5. All praise for Jesus, best gift divine
through word and witness, in bread and wine;
incarnate love song of boundless grace,
priest, teacher, prophet in time and space,
your steadfast kindness with human face:
Soli Deo gloria! Soli Deo gloria!

6. A billion voices in one great song,
now soft and gentle, now deep and strong,
in ev'ry culture and style and key,
from hill and valley, with sky and sea,
with Christ we praise you eternally:
Soli Deo gloria! Soli Deo gloria!

Text: Marty Haugen, b. 1950
Music: SOLI DEO GLORIA 9 9 9 9 9 and refrain, Marty Haugen
Text and music © 1999 GIA Publications, Inc. All rights reserved.

Acknowledgments

New Hymnody editorial team: Michael Burk, Cheryl Dieter, Pablo Espinoza, M. Alexandra George, Mark Glaeser, Karen Johnson-Lefsrud, Timothy Guenther, Mary Preus, Martin Seltz, Frank Stoldt, Scott Weidler, Wayne Wold

New Hymnody development panel: Norma Aamodt-Nelson, Donald Brandt, Susan Briehl, Lorraine Brugh, Gerhard Cartford, Marilyn Comer, Carl P. Daw Jr., Rusty Edwards, David Eicher, David Halaas, Marty Haugen, C. Michael Hawn, Robert Hobby, Gordon Lathrop, Debbie Lou Ludolph, Fred Ludolph, Rafael Malpica, Madeleine Forell Marshall, Angel Mattos, Mark Mummert, Peter Rehwaldt, Robert Rimbo, Thomas Schattauer, Amy Schifrin, Marilyn Stulken, Karen Walhof, Paul Westermeyer

Renewing Worship Songbook editorial production: Robert Buckley Farlee, Jessica Hillstrom, Becky Lowe, Mark Weiler

The publisher gratefully acknowledges all copyright holders who have granted permission to reproduce copyrighted materials in this book. Every effort has been made to determine the owner(s) and/or administrator(s) of each copyright and to secure needed permission. The publisher will, upon written notice, make necessary corrections in subsequent printings.

Permission to reproduce copyrighted words or music contained in this volume must be obtained from the copyright holder(s) of that material. A list of copyright holders that are publishers and institutions follows on the next pages, with information current as of the first date of this publication. For contact information of copyright holders not listed here or for further copyright information, please contact Augsburg Fortress.

Copyright Holders

Amity Music Corp.
1474 Gaylord Ter
Teaneck NJ 07666-6040
(201) 833-4808
Fax: (212) 720-7847

Asian Institute for Liturgy and Music
PO Box 10533
Broadway Centrum
Quezon City 1141
Philippines
(63) 2 722 8575
(63) 2 722 5554
Fax: (63) 2 722 1490
fffsama@pacific.net.ph

Augsburg Fortress
PO Box 1209
Minneapolis MN 55440-1209
(800) 421-0239 or (612) 330-3127
Fax: (612) 330-3252
copyright@augsburgfortress.org

Boosey & Hawkes, Inc.
35 E 21st St
New York NY 10010
(212) 358-5300
Fax: (212) 358-5305

Borealis Music
14409 Cartwright Ave
RR#3, Site 38,Comp 23
Summerland BC V0H 1Z0
Canada
(250) 494-5111
Fax: (250) 494-5139
LG@LinneaGood.com

Celebration
PO Box 309
Aliquippa PA 15001
(724) 375-1510
Fax: (724) 375-1138

Changing Church Forum, Inc./Prince of Peace Publishing
13901 Fairview Dr
Burnsville MN 55337
(952) 435-8107
(800) 784-2044
Fax: (952) 435-8065
changing@changingchurch.org

Chinese Christian Literature Council Ltd.
138 Nathan Road
4F.A
Kowloon, Hong Kong
China

Christian Conference of Asia
96, 2nd District, Pak Tin Village
Mei Tin Road
Shatin, Hong Kong
China
(852) 2691 1068
Fax: (852) 2692 4378 ext. 3805
cca@pacific.net.hk

Church Publishing Incorporated
445 Fifth Ave
New York NY 10016
(800) 223-6602 ext. 360
Fax: (212) 779-3392
churchpublishing@cpg.org

Concordia Publishing House
3558 S Jefferson Ave
St. Louis MO 63118-3968
(314) 268-1000
(800) 325-0191 (permissions)
Fax: (314) 268-1329
copyrights@cphnet.org

Desert Flower Music
Box 1476
Carmichael CA 95069

Doubleday
1540 Broadway
New York NY 10036
(212) 782-8957
Fax: (212) 782 8898

Earthsongs
220 NW 29th St
Corvallis OR 97330
(541) 758-5760
Fax: (541) 754-5887
email@earthsongsmus.com

EMI Christian Music Publishing
PO Box 5085
101 Winners Circle
Brentwood TN 37024-5085
(615) 371-6800
Fax: (615) 371-6897
dbolen@emicmg.com

GIA Publications, Inc.
7404 S Mason Ave
Chicago IL 60638
(708) 496-3800
(800) 442-1358
Fax: (708) 496-3828
custserv@giamusic.com

Hodder & Stoughton Ltd.
338 Euston Road
London NW1 3BH
United Kingdom
(44) 20 7873 6000
Fax: (44) 20 7873 6024

Hope Publishing Company
380 S Main Pl
Carol Stream IL 60188
(800) 323-1049
(630) 665-3200
Fax: (630) 665-2552

Integrity Music, Inc.
1000 Cody Rd
Mobile AL 36695
(251) 633-9000
Fax: (251) 633-5202

JASRAC
3-6-12 Uehara
Shibuya-ku
151-8540 Tokyo
Japan
(81) 3 3481 2121
Fax: (81) 3 3481 2150

Les Petites Soeurs de Jésus
Via Acque Salvie, 2
Tre Fontane
1-00142 Roma
Italy
(39) 06 592 54 25
Fax: (39) 06 591 26 57

Lilly Mack Music
421 E Beach
Inglewood CA 90302
(310) 677-5603
Fax: (310) 677-0250

Lorenz Publishing Corp.
PO Box 802
Dayton OH 45401-0802
(937) 228-6118
(800) 444-1144
Fax: (937) 223-2042

Malaco Records
PO Box 9287
Jackson MS 39286-9287
(601) 982-4522
Fax: (601) 982-4528
or Fax: (601) 362-1664

Manna Music, Inc.
35255 Brooten Rd
Box 218
Pacific City OR 97135
(503) 965-6112
Fax: (503) 965-6880
pcmannamusic@juno.com

Music Services, Inc.
209 Chapelwood Dr
Franklin TN 37069
(615) 794-9015
Fax: (615) 794-0793

Norsk Musikforlag
Karl Johans Gate 3
PO Box 1499 Vika
N-0116 Oslo 1
Norway
(47) 23 00 20 10
Fax: (47) 23 00 20 11

Oregon Catholic Press (OCP)
PO Box 18030
Portland OR 97218-0030
(503) 281-1191
(800) 548-8749
Fax: (503) 282-3486

Oxford University Press (New York)
198 Madison Ave
New York NY 10016-4314
(212) 726 6000
(800) 334 4249
Fax: (212) 726 6444
or Fax: (212) 726 6449

PeerMusic International
P.O. Box 10192
San Juan Station PR 00908-1192
(787) 723-5704
Fax: (787) 723-4381

Pilgrim Press/United Church Press
700 Prospect Ave E
Cleveland OH 44115-1100
(216) 736-3764
Fax: (216) 736-3703
pilgrim@ucc.org or ucpress@ucc.org

Selah Publishing Co.
58 Pearl St
Box 3037
Kingston NY 12401-0902
(845) 338-2816
Fax: (845) 338-2991
www.selahpub.com

Sisters of St. Benedict
St. Benedict's Monastery
104 Chapel Lane
St. Joseph MN 56374

The Copyright Company
1025 16th Avenue South, Suite 204
Nashville TN 37212
(615) 321-1096
Fax: (615) 321-1099
tcc@thecopyrightco.com

Unichappell Music Inc.
c/o Hal Leonard Corporation
7777 W Bluemound Rd
Box 13819
Milwaukee WI 53213
(414) 774-3630
Fax: (414) 774-3259

Word Music Group, Inc.
c/o Warner/Chapell Music
20 Music Square East
Nashville TN 37203
(615) 733-1880
Fax: (615) 733-1885

World Council of Churches (Switzerland)
150 route de Ferney
P.O. Box 2100
CH-1211 Geneva 2
Switzerland
(41) 22 791 6111
Fax: (41) 22 791 0361

Topical and Seasonal Index

COMMITMENT, R274–R283

R148   Christ Is Risen! Shout Hosanna!
R132   Eternal Lord of Love, Behold Your Church
R154   Fire of God, Undying Flame
R199   Give Me a Clean Heart
R207   I Heard the Voice of Jesus Say
R163   I'm Going on a Journey
R141   O Dearest Lord, Your Sacred Head
R260   O God in Heaven
R153   Send Down the Fire
R160   Song over the Waters
R189   The Lord Now Sends Us Forth
R226   There Is a Name I Love to Hear
R164   This Is the Spirit's Entry Now
R161   Waterlife
R237   When Pain of the World Surrounds Us

*Communion of Saints—See Christian Hope,
Heaven/Eternal Life*

COMMUNITY IN CHRIST, R211–R222 *(See also Unity)*

R241   A Place at the Table
R129   Bless Now, O God, the Journey
R168   By Your Hand You Feed Your People
R101   Come Now, O Prince of Peace
R149   Day of Arising
R170   I Come with Joy
R223   In Christ Called to Baptize
R178   Let Us Go Now to the Banquet
R247   O Christ, Your Heart, Compassionate
R294   Praise the One Who Breaks the Darkness
R162   Remember and Rejoice
R145   The Risen Christ
R175   United at the Table
R161   Waterlife
R251   We Are Called
R184   What Is This Place

Confession, Forgiveness—See Forgiveness/Healing

Confirmation—See Affirmation of Baptism

CREATION/PRESERVATION, R252–R256

R298   Come, Join the Dance of Trinity
R193   Joyous Light of Heavenly Glory
R124   Light Shone in Darkness
R296   Shout to the Lord

Death—See Heaven/Eternal Life, Christian Hope, Burial

Earth—See Creation/Preservation

EASTER, R145–R151

R177   Bread of Life from Heaven
R239   Goodness Is Stronger than Evil
R121   Oh, Sing a Song of Bethlehem

Easter, Vigil of

R136   As the Deer Runs to the River
R158   Crashing Waters at Creation
R163   I'm Going on a Journey
R159   Wade in the Water
R172   Welcome Table

EPIPHANY, R121–R128

R113   Midnight Stars Make Bright the Sky
R251   We Are Called

Eternal Life—See Heaven/Eternal Life

Evening

R146   Alleluia! Christ Is Arisen
R245   Canticle of the Turning
R127   Christ, Be Our Light
R149   Day of Arising
R193   Joyous Light of Heavenly Glory
R195   Lord, Support Us All Day Long
R107   Magnificat
R196   My Heart Sings Out with Joyful Praise
R194   Now It Is Evening

Expanded Images for God

R216   Bring Many Names
R255   God the Sculptor of the Mountains
R108   Unexpected and Mysterious

Faith

R146   Alleluia! Christ Is Arisen
R129   Bless Now, O God, the Journey
R206   Lord, It Belongs Not to My Care
R202   Neither Death Nor Life
R173   Soul, Adorn Yourself with Gladness
R227   This Is the Threefold Truth
R269   We've Come This Far by Faith

FORGIVENESS/HEALING, R197–R199

R136   As the Deer Runs to the River
R183   As We Gather at Your Table
R127   Christ, Be Our Light
R101   Come Now, O Prince of Peace
R267   Come to Me, All Pilgrims Thirsty
R200   Come, Ye Disconsolate
R135   God Loved the World
R179   Here, O Lord, Your Servants Gather
R134   Lamb of God
R277   Lord Jesus, You Shall Be My Song
R113   Midnight Stars Make Bright the Sky
R157   O Christ, What Can It Mean for Us
R294   Praise the One Who Breaks the Darkness
R133   Restore in Us, O God
R105   The King of Glory
R108   Unexpected and Mysterious

Freedom

R123   Christ, When for Us You Were Baptized
R300   Soli Deo Gloria
R246   When Our Song Says Peace

Funerals—See Burial, Christian Hope, Heaven/Eternal Life

GATHERING, R178–R185

R227   This Is the Threefold Truth

Good Friday

R143   Calvary
R141   O Dearest Lord, Your Sacred Head
R144   They Crucified My Lord
R142   When I Survey the Wondrous Cross

Light

Love

Marriage

Mary, Mother of Our Lord

Maundy Thursday

Mission—See Witness

Morning

MORNING/EVENING, R192–R196 *(See also Morning, Evening)*

Offertory

Palm Sunday—See Sunday of the Passion

Peace

PENTECOST/THE HOLY SPIRIT, R152–R154

PRAISE/ADORATION, R284–R300

PRAYER, R257–R261

Reconciliation—See Forgiveness/Healing

Repentance—See Forgiveness/Healing

Text and Music Sources

Tunes—Alphabetical

Titles and First Lines

ISBN 080667050-9

Augsburg Fortress

www.renewingworship.org